Teach Yourself
VISUALLY™
Digital Photography, 3rd Edition

Visual

by Dave Huss and Lynette Kent

WILEY

Wiley Publishing, Inc.

Teach Yourself VISUALLY™ Digital Photography, 3rd Edition

Published by
Wiley Publishing, Inc.
111 River Street
Hoboken, NJ 07030-5774

Published simultaneously in Canada

Library of Congress Control Number: 2005931149

ISBN-13: 978-0-7645-9941-5

ISBN-10: 0-7645-9941-0

Manufactured in the United States of America

10 9 8 7 6 5 4 3 2 1

Trademark Acknowledgments

Wiley, the Wiley Publishing logo, Visual, the Visual logo, Simplified, Master VISUALLY, Teach Yourself VISUALLY, Visual Blueprint, Read Less-Learn More, and related trade dress are trademarks or registered trademarks of John Wiley & Sons, Inc. and/or its affiliates. All other trademarks are the property of their respective owners. Wiley Publishing, Inc. is not associated with any product or vendor mentioned in this book.

Contact Us

For general information on our other products and services please contact our Customer Care Department within the U.S. at 800-762-2974, outside the U.S. at 317-572-3993, or fax 317-572-4002.

For technical support please visit www.wiley.com/techsupport.

Wiley Publishing, Inc.

U.S. Sales

Contact Wiley
at (800) 762-2974 or
fax (317) 572-4002.

Praise for Visual Books

"Like a lot of other people, I understand things best when I see them visually. Your books really make learning easy and life more fun."

John T. Frey (Cadillac, MI)

"I have quite a few of your Visual books and have been very pleased with all of them. I love the way the lessons are presented!"

Mary Jane Newman (Yorba Linda, CA)

"I just purchased my third Visual book (my first two are dog-eared now!), and, once again, your product has surpassed my expectations.

Tracey Moore (Memphis, TN)

"I am an avid fan of your Visual books. If I need to learn anything, I just buy one of your books and learn the topic it in no time. Wonders! I have even trained my friends to give me Visual books as gifts."

Illona Bergstrom (Aventura, FL)

"Thank you for making it so clear. I appreciate it. I will buy many more Visual books."

J.P. Sangdong (North York, Ontario, Canada)

"I have several books from the Visual series and have always found them to be valuable resources."

Stephen P. Miller (Ballston Spa, NY)

"Thank you for the wonderful books you produce. It wasn't until I was an adult that I discovered how I learn – visually. Nothing compares to Visual books. I love the simple layout. I can just grab a book and use it at my computer, lesson by lesson. And I understand the material! You really know the way I think and learn. Thanks so much!"

Stacey Han (Avondale, AZ)

"I absolutely admire your company's work. Your books are terrific. The format is perfect, especially for visual learners like me. Keep them coming!"

Frederick A. Taylor, Jr. (New Port Richey, FL)

"I have several of your Visual books and they are the best I have ever used."

Stanley Clark (Crawfordville, FL)

"I bought my first Teach Yourself VISUALLY book last month. Wow. Now I want to learn everything in this easy format!"

Tom Vial (New York, NY)

"Thank you, thank you, thank you...for making it so easy for me to break into this high-tech world. I now own four of your books. I recommend them to anyone who is a beginner like myself."

Gay O'Donnell (Calgary, Alberta, Canada)

"I write to extend my thanks and appreciation for your books. They are clear, easy to follow, and straight to the point. Keep up the good work! I bought several of your books and they are just right! No regrets! I will always buy your books because they are the best."

Seward Kollie (Dakar, Senegal)

"Compliments to the chef!! Your books are extraordinary! Or, simply put, extra-ordinary, meaning way above the rest! THANKYOU THANKYOU THANKYOU! I buy them for friends, family, and colleagues."

Christine J. Manfrin (Castle Rock, CO)

"What fantastic teaching books you have produced! Congratulations to you and your staff. You deserve the Nobel Prize in Education in the Software category. Thanks for helping me understand computers."

Bruno Tonon (Melbourne, Australia)

"Over time, I have bought a number of your 'Read Less - Learn More' books. For me, they are THE way to learn anything easily. I learn easiest using your method of teaching."

José A. Mazón (Cuba, NY)

"I am an avid purchaser and reader of the Visual series, and they are the greatest computer books I've seen. The Visual books are perfect for people like myself who enjoy the computer, but want to know how to use it more efficiently. Your books have definitely given me a greater understanding of my computer, and have taught me to use it more effectively. Thank you very much for the hard work, effort, and dedication that you put into this series."

Alex Diaz (Las Vegas, NV)

Oct 04

Credits

Project Editor
Sarah Hellert

Acquisitions Editor
Jody Lefevere

Product Development Supervisor
Courtney Allen

Copy Editor
Tricia Liebig

Technical Editor
Ron Rockwell

Editorial Manager
Robyn Siesky

Manufacturing
Allan Conley
Linda Cook
Paul Gilchrist
Jennifer Guynn

Book Design
Kathie Rickard

Production Coordinator
Adrienne Martinez

Layout
Beth Brooks
Jennifer Heleine
Amanda Spagnuolo

Screen Artist
Jill A. Proll

Illustrators
Steven Amory
Matthew Bell
Elizabeth Cardenas-Nelson
Kristin Corley
Ronda David-Burroughs
Cheryl Grubbs
Sean Johanessen
Jacob Mansfield
Rita Marley
Paul Schmitt III

Proofreader
Laura L. Bowman

Quality Control
Joe Niesen

Indexer
Joan Griffitts

Vice President and Executive Group Publisher
Richard Swadley

Vice President and Publisher
Barry Pruett

Director of Composition Services
Debbie Stailey

About the Authors

Dave Huss is a photographer with 40 years of experience. He has taught classes in digital photography and photo editing in the U.S. and Europe, and his numerous books on these topics have been translated into six languages. He has been honored frequently for his photo work, receiving awards in international competitions including the Grand Prize for his photomontage work at the Corel International Design Contest. A contributing editor for *Photoshop User* magazine, he has also appeared on CNN and TechTV.

Lynette Kent studied art and French at Stanford University. After completing her master's degree, she taught at both the high school and community college level. In addition to writing books and magazine articles, Lynette works as a demo artist for computer hardware and software companies, and helps lead the Adobe Technology Exchange of Southern California, a professional organization for designers, photographers, and artists. She spends her free time painting, both with the computer and with traditional media, and shooting photos.

Authors' Acknowledgments

Dave Huss – Many thanks to the Photoshop Elements development team, particularly Mark Dahm. It was a joy to work with my good friend Lynette Kent on this book. I want to thank acquisitions editor Jody Lefevere, who put the parts of the book together; project editor Sarah Hellert for her patience; copy editor Tricia Liebig for her attention to detail; and technical editor Ron Rockwell for his valuable input. I especially want to thank all of the people that let me use their pictures in the book. I must also include thanks to my family, who puts up with my absences while I write books.

Lynette Kent – Special thanks to author/photographer Dave Huss and acquisitions editor Jody Lefevere for asking me to contribute to this book; to project editor Sarah Hellert for her meticulous unscrambling of chapters; to copy editor Tricia Liebig for making sure the text was legible; and to technical editor Ron Rockwell for overseeing the accuracy of the often complicated terminology. Special thanks to Rick Redfern for helping me explain the world of color, and as always, to my parents.

Table of Contents

chapter 4   Controlling Exposure and Focal Length

chapter 5   Learning About Focus

Table of Contents

Table of Contents

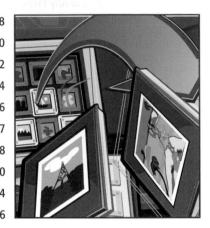

chapter 12 Fixing Photos

chapter 13 Enhancing Photos

Table of Contents

chapter 14 **Getting Creative with Photoshop Elements**

chapter 15 · Printing Photos and Other Projects

chapter 16 · Sharing Photos Electronically

CHAPTER 1

Understanding Digital Photography

Are you confused about how digital photography works? This chapter introduces you to the advantages of digital photography, the different types of digital cameras, and how easy it is to work with and use digital pictures.

Why Go Digital?

With digital photography, you can do more than take snapshots for your family album. You can use a digital camera to quickly and significantly improve your photography skills. You can e-mail your digital pictures to family and friends, or create interesting Web pages about your hobbies, family, or even home business. You can also simplify everyday tasks, or take part in the popular hobby of documenting your family history with a digital scrapbook.

Improve Your Photography Skills

Because digital pictures do not require film and processing, you can experiment with lighting, composition, camera modes, and creative techniques at no cost. Because you see images immediately, if an experiment yields poor results, you can delete the picture, modify your setting or approach, and try again. The best way to become a better photographer is to take many pictures.

Simplify Everyday Tasks

A digital camera allows you to share and convey information easily. For example, you can capture special moments such as birthdays and anniversaries and almost immediately send the pictures to your friends in an e-mail message, or post them on a Web site. You can also take digital pictures of club members for a visual directory. Other tasks include creating a home inventory for insurance records, and photographing items you are selling on eBay.

Share Pictures Online and in E-mail

Within minutes of taking a picture, you can share it in an e-mail message, or upload it to an online photo site to share with family and friends. By doing it this way, those loved ones who want prints of the photos can buy them online and receive the prints in the mail.

Create Photo Slide Shows on CDs or DVDs

You can use programs, such as Photoshop Elements, to create digital image slide shows on recordable CDs and DVDs. Then you can add voice narration, captions, music, digital movie clips, and transitions to finish the slide show. Photoshop Elements also lets you organize your digital images by assigning each photo a *keyword*. If you like, you can even add a *rating*, which is similar to the star ratings that are so popular with movies and hotels. You can use these keywords or ratings to find and select a particular photo for your slide show or just see all your best photos with a click of a button.

When you understand how digital cameras work, you can take that knowledge and make an informed decision when it comes time to purchase your first digital camera or to upgrade your existing one. Knowing how digital cameras work also allows you to get better images from your camera.

How Digital Cameras Record Pictures

Digital cameras record pictures using an *image sensor array* — a grid composed of millions of light-sensitive *pixels*. The term pixel describes a picture element. The pixels are the building blocks of all digital images. A red, green, or blue filter covers each pixel on the sensor so that it responds to only one of the primary colors of light. Each pixel reads the brightness and color in a scene to produce an electrical signal. The signal is then converted to a digital number that represents the color and brightness of the pixel. The camera's onboard computer processes the information to build a final image before storing it in memory.

Types of Image Sensors

Most digital cameras use one of two types of image sensors: a Charge-Coupled Device (CCD), or a Complementary Metal-Oxide Semiconductor (CMOS). Although there are technical differences between them, both produce high-quality images.

Resolution and Image Quality

Resolution is a measure of pixel density; the higher the resolution, the more pixels there are in every inch and the greater detail that is possible in the image. On a digital camera, the greater the number of pixels on the image sensor, the larger you can print the photo. There are consumer cameras with sensor sizes up to 8 megapixels. If most of your images are 4 by 6 or sent by e-mail, any digital camera with a sensor of 3 megapixels or greater can produce prints large enough for all your needs.

A digital workflow is a step-by-step process that helps you get the best digital images and also manages your collection of images. The workflow includes taking, editing, sharing, organizing, and storing digital pictures. You can use the digital workflow described here as an introduction to and ongoing guide for working with your digital images.

Capture Images

The digital workflow begins by choosing camera settings that will produce the best photo. You can choose a preset scene mode (portrait, landscape, or sunset, for example), use a fully automatic setting, or set the camera to operate in manual shooting mode.

Change the white balance to match the light in the scene. For more information on white balance, see Chapter 8.

Then adjust zoom, compose the image in the frame, ensure the autofocus has the subject in focus, and take the picture. To learn more about exposure, see Chapter 4.

Verify Exposure and Composition

Next, review the picture on the camera's LCD screen to ensure that the exposure and composition are acceptable. If the picture is too light (overexposed), too dark (underexposed), or has highlight areas with no detail, adjust the exposure using exposure compensation. As you review the image on your LCD, look for distracting background elements, closed eyes, and other elements that you can improve. When in doubt, retake the picture — as many times as you want — it is free.

Use the LCD

The camera's LCD provides too small of a view to know if a picture is good or not. If possible, zoom the LCD display to get a better idea of the overall quality. Unless the picture is hopelessly flawed, you should not delete it. Instead, wait and evaluate it on your computer — you may be able to save the shot.

Transfer Pictures to a Computer

You can transfer pictures from your camera to your computer with a USB cable, a card reader, or a docking station. The fastest way to transfer pictures is by using a card reader. Card readers come in many forms, they are cheap, and they do not drain your camera battery — which happens when you hook your camera to the computer. See Chapter 8 to learn more about working with digital images.

continued

Edit Pictures

You can use image editing software that comes with your camera or computer, or software that you purchase to edit pictures. Image editing programs enable you to rotate, adjust color and saturation, correct red eye, remove unwanted elements (ex-boyfriends), crop, resize, sharpen, combine, and add text to digital pictures. See Chapters 12 and 13 to learn more about working with image editing software.

Print and Share Pictures

After you edit, size, and sharpen your pictures, you can print them on a home photo-quality printer, or at a commercial printing service. You can also share them in e-mail messages or on a photo-sharing Web site. For more information about printing and sharing pictures, see Chapters 15 and 16.

Organize and Store Digital Negatives

You should not alter the original image, which is the equivalent of a film negative. If you need to make changes to an image, get in the habit of making changes to a copy and keeping the original file untouched. This is not as hard as it sounds. Some image editors automatically apply your changes to a copy rather than to the original.

The best way to manage your picture collection (which will become very large) is to use one of the many photo organizer programs that are available. Many users think that they will not need one when they begin taking photographs only to discover their collection has grown to an unmanageable size in a short period of time. You can always find a particular photo quickly without spending hours searching for it if you consistently assign keywords and descriptions to your photos using programs such as Photo Organizer in Photoshop Elements or Paint Shop Album.

Clear the Memory Card

After your pictures are on your computer, you can safely delete pictures from your memory card. Many image editors offer to delete pictures after they have been transferred, but you should be sure that the images have been successfully placed on your hard drive because when the images are deleted from the card, you cannot get them back. Allowing the image editor to delete the photos usually works fine, but the optimum choice is to format the card using your camera. The card format option is typically found as a menu option that is accessed from the menu on the LCD screen of your camera.

CHAPTER 2

What You Need to Get Started

Knowing the basics about digital cameras, resolution, lenses, batteries, and accessories helps you choose the camera that is right for you. Having the right equipment for your digital darkroom enables you to edit and print your images.

Choose a Digital Camera

When choosing a digital camera, consider the size of the camera, the resolution, how much control you want to have over the camera settings, the quality and focal range of the lens, the shooting modes you use most often, the life of the battery, and the type of storage media available.

Compact

Compact, or point-and-shoot, digital cameras typically capture photos with image resolutions ranging from 1 to 5 megapixels (millions of pixels). They include a built-in flash and zoom. Although compact cameras offer few, if any, manual controls, they often provide a number of handy shooting presets that allow you to optimize the settings for better pictures.

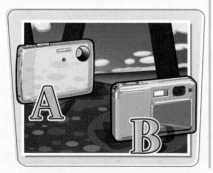

Advanced Non-SLR Cameras

Advanced non-SLR (single lens reflex) digital camera resolution ranges from 4 to 8 megapixels. Also called *prosumer* (professional/consumer) cameras, they feature more exposure control and greater zoom ranges than compact cameras but are also larger, heavier, and more expensive. Some offer wide-angle and telephoto accessory lenses.

Digital SLR

Resolutions for a digital SLR (D-SLR) camera range from 4 to 22 megapixels. These cameras offer all the features and controls found on film SLR cameras. The choice of professional photographers, D-SLR cameras offer a wide variety of detachable lenses and can cost more than a late-model used car.

Lens Considerations

Most compact cameras come with a 3× zoom lens in the 38mm to 105mm range. Look for the largest *optical* (not digital) zoom factor you can afford. The optical zoom factor is the amount of magnification that is produced by the internal lenses in the camera. The digital zoom is created by enlarging the pixels that make up the image, producing an image that appears slightly out of focus and grainy. The zoom number of a digital camera is typically displayed in bold letters on the camera and its box. Do not be fooled by zoom numbers that are a combination of optical and digital zoom factors. The drawback of a large optical zoom is that it makes the camera physically larger. You can learn more about lenses in Chapter 4.

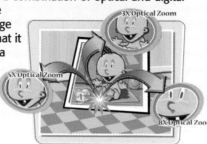

Evaluate Exposure and Scene Modes

As a baseline, look for a camera that includes automatic and semiautomatic exposure modes. Most compact cameras include scene modes that automatically set the camera's focal length, shutter speed, and flash based on the scene mode that you choose. Advanced non-SLR cameras include semiautomatic and manual controls, and most include scene modes.

Batteries

Depending on the model, digital cameras use disposable, rechargeable, or product-specific batteries. Some cameras can use disposable and rechargeable batteries interchangeably. This is convenient because you can use disposable batteries when you cannot recharge your batteries and use rechargeable batteries all other times. Always buy the right type of battery, and get at least two sets of batteries to ensure uninterrupted shooting.

Storage Media

Digital cameras store pictures on removable memory media, such as a Secure Digital (SD), CompactFlash (CF), or Memory Stick. Storage media, commonly referred to as memory cards, comes in a variety of sizes and has a variety of uses including MP3 players, cell phones, and PDAs (Personal Data Assistants). If you currently have one of these, you should consider a camera that uses the same media so you can share them between the devices and your camera. The size you need depends on the resolution of your camera, and the type you need depends on the camera you buy. The best size to buy is the one that is a few sizes down from the current maximum capacity of the media. When a new larger size is introduced, the former top cards drop dramatically in price.

Consider Digital Camera Accessories

Although most digital cameras come with everything you need to take your first pictures, you can add helpful accessories. Accessories include higher-capacity memory cards, a card reader, extra or better batteries, an accessory flash, accessory lenses, and a tripod.

Photo Storage Devices

If you are taking your camera with you on an extended vacation, you may need to consider a photo storage device. You can transfer your pictures off of the memory card to the storage device, freeing up the memory card. These devices come in a variety of shapes and prices. Some are MP3 players that provide the option of storing photos; others are designed specifically to store and preview photos. An alternative is to buy a notebook computer with a small screen. Because its primary use would be as a storage device, the laptop could be an older, slower laptop model that you could get relatively inexpensively.

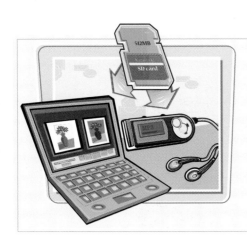

Memory Card Capacity

The number of images a memory card can hold depends on the resolution of the camera, and the file format and compression you set using the image-quality menu on the camera. Memory cards are relatively cheap. Get a few that are at least 256MB. To see how much it will hold on your camera, plug it in and format the card. To learn more about image resolution, file formats, and compression, see Chapter 1.

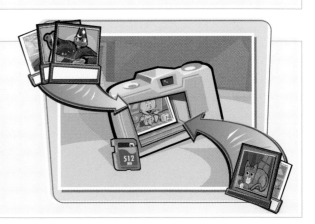

Card Readers

You can easily transfer pictures from your camera to your computer using a USB cable or camera dock. However, a memory card reader provides a fast and inexpensive way to transfer images. Most card readers connect to the computer using a USB cable, and some card readers accept multiple types of memory cards. These card readers are named for the number of different types of memory cards that can be used with them. The more common readers are called 9-way or 11-way readers, and the newest card readers are 19-way readers. For owners of a notebook computer, there are PCMCIA (PC Card) readers that are memory media specific.

Accessory Lenses

If your camera accepts accessory lenses, the lenses offer you additional photography flexibility and are typically wide-angle or telephoto lenses. Look for accessory lenses from the manufacturer of your camera and from aftermarket suppliers. Most accessory lenses require step-up or step-down rings. The ring attaches to the camera's lens, and then the accessory lens attaches to the other side of the ring.

Accessory Flash Unit

If your camera has a flash mount, or *hot shoe,* you can add an external flash unit. The advantage of an external flash is that it has more power offering greater distances for flash shots. Because it is higher above the camera, it dramatically reduces red eye in the photos that you take. To learn more about lighting and flash photography, see Chapter 3.

Travel Accessories

If you are traveling to another country, check what power and power connectors are used in that country. If you are sure your battery charger works with that power, check for the proper adapter. Voltage is rarely a problem but frequency is. A charger that only works on 60Hz will burn out in a few minutes if plugged into a 50Hz power outlet. So it is best to have one that works on 50/60Hz plus have the proper power connection for the country you are visiting.

continued

Tripods

You can take sharp pictures in lower-light scenes if your camera is absolutely stable, and if the subject does not move. You can stabilize your camera by using a tripod. Tripods range from small tabletop versions, which are suitable for small digital cameras, to full-size tripods suitable for large digital cameras. Look for a solid, well-built tripod.

Camera and Accessory Bag

Also consider buying a weather-resistant camera bag. Bags range in size from small pouches to full-size bags with compartments for flash units, lenses, and spare batteries.

If you will be traveling on vacation, avoid using a camera bag with your camera brand emblazoned on it. It will attract thieves. Consider instead using a diaper bag for your camera gear. They are inexpensive (you may already own one), have lots of pockets, and no thief will give it a second look.

To protect easy-to-lose memory cards, you can buy hard- or soft-sided memory card cases that hold two or more memory cards.

Filters

Although digital cameras do not require color correction filters, some traditional filters, including a *UV filter*, can protect the lens of some digital cameras. You can also use a *polarizing* filter on some digital cameras (if the camera lens had threads to accept a filter) to reduce reflections and to make colors more vibrant. If you are buying a polarizer filter, make sure it says "circular polarizer" on the filter case. Linear (noncircular) polarizer filters confuse autofocus systems.

Creative Filters

You can use filters to add starbursts and halo effects to lights. A *diffuser* filter creates a light fog effect by using a soft focus. Color filters alter the color of your picture. You can also reproduce the effects of some creative filters in most image editing software.

Cleaning Supplies

To clean your lens, you can use microfiber lens-cleaning cloths and a blower brush. You can also use a lens pen. A *lens pen* has a brush on one end to sweep away particles, and a circular pad with lens-cleaning fluid to wipe away smudges on the other end.

Build a Digital Darkroom

Unlike film photography, digital cameras do not require chemicals and a room without light to develop photos. Your digital equivalent of a darkroom is your computer in combination with your image editing software and maybe even your photo printer. Armed with this equipment, you can ensure that your pictures have great color and contrast, and that they are precisely cropped. To create this virtual digital darkroom, you need a computer, monitor, and software for editing images.

Computer

Digital photo files and photo editing tasks require more hard drive space and RAM than text files and processing require. To speed up digital photography work, it is helpful to have a computer with sufficient RAM (at least 256MB), a hard drive with free space to store photos, and a reasonably large monitor that you can calibrate for accurate color.

Minimum System Requirements

A good way to determine if your computer RAM and hard drive space is adequate for image editing is to check the system requirements for both the image editing program and the operating system. You can find this information on the software product box.

System Requirements
- Intel® Pentium® III
- Windows XP
- RAM: 256MB
- Display: 1024x768
  Continue

CD or DVD Archiving

As your digital image collection grows, it is good practice to archive images on CDs or DVDs. A recordable CD stores 700MB at a cost of 10 cents or less per CD. A recordable DVD stores 4.7GB of data. DVD prices vary by brand and DVD format, but they cost little more than CDs. The newest high-capacity storage is Dual Layer (DL) DVD, which offers more than 8GB of storage. Unfortunately, the DL blank media is quite expensive, but its price should go down after it becomes more popular.

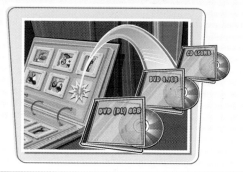

Recordable CD and DVD Media

A *CD–R* or a *DVD–R, DVD+R,* or *DVD–R* disc allows you to write to the CD/DVD once and read from the CD/DVD repeatedly. A *CD–RW, DVD+RW, DVD–RW,* or *DVD–RAM* disc allows you to write to, erase, and read from the CD/DVD repeatedly, much like a floppy disk. CD–R and DVD–R discs are less expensive than CD–RW and DVD rewritable discs, but they cannot be reused.

Choose an Image Editing Program

An image editing program allows you to adjust the contrast and color, and to rotate, crop, and add text and special effects to your pictures. In addition to basic image editing, most software helps you organize your images, e-mail them to friends, print them, and even help you assemble impressive slide shows — which can be used for digital scrapbooking.

Monitor Types, Sizes, and Settings

Both CRTs and LCD flat-panels display digital images accurately. CRTs are quickly going the way of 8-track tapes. Nearly all displays sold today are flat-panel displays. A 15-inch computer monitor is adequate, but a 17-inch or larger monitor provides additional photo-viewing space. Screen resolution should be at least 1024 × 768 pixels. Digital photo editing requires that the color depth be set to 24- or 32-bit depending on your graphics adapter. If you purchased your computer in the last few years, it is already set up at an adequate resolution and color-depth setting.

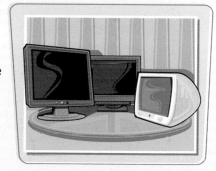

High-quality, affordable photo printers along with premium photo paper enable you to easily print your own photos that are indistinguishable from your photo developer's. You can choose from a wide variety of dedicated photo printers that produce fade-resistant prints in a large variety of sizes. Most printers also sell a diverse selection of media ranging from preprinted cards to museum-quality paper, for those special photos.

Inkjet Printers

Inkjet printers, the most common printer type, use four or more ink colors. They spray tiny droplets of colored ink (usually organic dyes) onto the paper to print the photo. Depending on the quality of the ink and paper, inkjet prints can last from several months to many years without fading.

Dye-Sublimation Printers

Dye-sublimation, or *dye-sub,* printers apply heat to a printer ribbon producing a colored gas that bonds with the paper to create the photo. Dye-sub printers produce continuous-tone prints that most closely resemble traditional film prints, and the print life is comparable to high-quality inkjet prints. The disadvantage of dye-sub printers is that they are very expensive to buy and to operate. The most common type of dye-sub printer is a small 4 by 6 printer, and on average, prints cost between 60 cents and 80 cents each.

Print Directly from Memory Media

Direct printing lets you print pictures without transferring pictures to your computer first. On some printers, you can insert the memory card into a slot, and then print all or some of the images. On direct-print printers, you can attach your digital camera to the printer using a USB cable, and then print all or part of the images.

Print Speed

Usually the print speed published by the manufacturer is for draft-quality printing, and not for the best photo-quality printing. Print speed is measured in pages per minute (PPM).

Paper Size

Printers commonly use 8.5 × 11-inch paper to print an 8 × 10.5-inch image. Some printers can print on 11 × 14-inch paper and larger paper sizes.

Connection

Most printers connect to the computer using a USB cable. Some professional printers use either a USB or a FireWire (1394) interface. If the printer has a USB 2.0 connection and your computer only has a USB 1.0/1.1 connection port, it will still work — just a little slower.

Cost

The manufacturer cost-per-print estimates are usually not figured at the best setting of the printer, which uses more ink. You should use manufacturer estimates for comparison only. Color print costs range from approximately 18 cents to $2 or more per 8 × 10-inch print. One way to get your cost down is not to print every image at the highest resolution. Save that for your better images and use lower resolution — and less ink — for the rest.

Print Quality

New inkjet printers usually offer a maximum color resolution of 4800 × 1200 dots per inch (dpi). When you evaluate printed samples from different printers, look for smooth, continuous tones, fine gradations of color, and color accuracy and fidelity.

CHAPTER 5

Understanding Light

Learn how to use light to create a mood or atmosphere, define a shape or a form, and bring out details in your photographs.

You can use the qualities of light to set the mood and to influence a viewer's emotional response to the picture. You can also use light to reveal or partially hide the subject's shape, form, texture, and detail, or use light to show colors in the scene as vibrant or subdued.

Light and Color

All colors within the color spectrum are contained in visible light. The amount of any particular color within the light is determined by its source, and for outdoor light, the time of day. For example, more reddish orange color is seen at sunset when the sun's low angle causes light to pass through more of the heated earth's atmosphere. Midday light on an overcast day produces a bluish color, while indoor light, such as candlelight and tungsten light bulbs, produces a reddish quality. Knowing how these different light sources affect your photographs will help you make more appealing ones.

Sunrise

Cobalt and purple hues of the night sky predominate during early sunrise. Within minutes, the landscape begins to reflect the warm gold and red hues of the sunrise. Early morning light is produced by sunlight passing through the atmosphere at a low angle, which means that the light is going through much more of the earth's atmosphere than it would if the sun was directly overhead. (This same increase in atmospheric layers has a magnifying effect, which explains why the sun and the moon appear so much larger when they are close to the horizon.) Later in the morning as the sun gets higher in the sky, the light shifts to a rich blue. Most photographers agree that the best shooting light for clear skies is an hour after sunrise until around 10 AM and then again when the sun is within a few hours of setting.

Midday

During midday, the warm and cool colors of light equalize to create a white or neutral light. Bright midday light produces harsh shadows and a bluish color cast making it unsuitable for some types of photography, particularly portraiture. Midday light works well for photographing shadow patterns, flower petals and plant leaves made translucent against the sun, and for natural and manmade structures such as rock formations and buildings.

Sunset

During the time just before, during, and just following sunset, the warmest and most intense color of natural light occurs. The predominantly red, yellow, and gold light creates vibrant colors, while the low angle of the sun creates soft contrasts that define and enhance textures and shapes. Sunset colors create rich landscape, cityscape, and wildlife photographs.

Electronic Flash

Most on-camera electronic flashes are balanced for the neutral (white) color of midday light, while others are balanced toward the cool end of the color spectrum. Electronic flash light is neutral, and in the correct intensities, reproduces colors accurately. On the negative side, using a flash can bring out unwanted details, such as wrinkles, and a flash can produce hard shadows (called cast shadows) behind the subject, as shown here.

Household or Candlelight

Tungsten is household light. Tungsten light, like firelight and candlelight, appears warmer than daylight and produces a yellow/orange cast in photos taken using a digital or a film camera. Although this color cast can be corrected, in many cases it is desirable, as shown in this interior photo of a California mission.

Fluorescent Light

Commonly found in office and public places, fluorescent light typically produces a green cast in photos taken using a digital camera that has the white balance set to daylight or auto. Typically this color cast is seldom seen in the photo because when the subject is lit by fluorescents, the light is low enough to cause the camera's automatic flash to fire. The flash produces sufficient light to overcome any color cast produced by the fluorescent lighting. In addition to fluorescent lighting, you need to be aware of high-pressure sodium lamps used to illuminate streets, large buildings, and arenas. To the human eye, the light they produce appears to have a slightly peach color cast but, the resulting digital photos usually have a greenish cast, as shown here.

Measure and Correct Light for Color

In film photography, the color composition of the light is controlled by attaching color filters in front of the lens to compensate for or enhance various ranges of color. This is because the color balance of the film is determined by its chemical composition and cannot be changed. Digital cameras allow you to control the color balance of the sensor by manually changing the White Balance (WB) setting.

How Light Color Is Measured

In photography, image color is measured as a temperature. Each color of light corresponds to a temperature measured on the Kelvin (K) scale in degrees. It works the opposite way that you would expect it to. The higher the temperature, the cooler (or more blue) the light. The lower the temperature, the warmer (or more yellow/red) the light. In short, subjects lit by higher temperature light appear cooler; when lit by cooler light, subjects appear warmer.

Light Meters

Not too long ago, all camera light meters assumed that everything you focused on was neutral gray, which reflects 18 percent of the light and absorbs the rest. Today, the 18 percent gray card is still used for calibrating the white balance setting of a digital camera. Some high-end digital cameras offer a white balance calibration feature. Unfortunately, calibrating the WB of a digital camera is only effective in a studio where the lighting does not change. When the light meter in a modern digital camera evaluates a scene, it reads hundreds of areas of light and dark in the image frame and adjusts the camera to capture the greatest amount of detail without over- or underexposing the image.

Why Correct for Light?

The human eye automatically adjusts to changing light color and sees white as being white in different types of light. Unfortunately, digital cameras do not adjust to color temperature changes like the human eye does. As the color temperature of the light illuminating the subject changes, so does the color cast on the finished photo. To achieve the desired color in a photo, either the white balance of the camera must be adjusted or the color of the photo must be corrected using the computer.

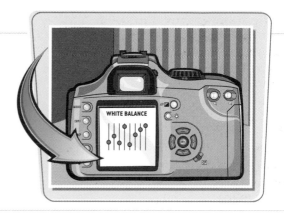

Automatic White Balance

There are several ways to achieve desired color rendition using a digital camera. You can manually set the white balance or let the camera set it for you automatically. Early digital cameras were not very good at calculating white balance automatically, but most modern digital cameras now do a good job.

Set White Balance

On digital cameras, you adjust the white balance to tell the camera the temperature or type of light in the scene. White balance options, such as Bright Sun, Tungsten, and Fluorescent, are set using one of the camera's menus. Choose the setting that matches the predominant light in the scene. Some cameras allow you to adjust settings with a + or – to get more precise color. Newer cameras offer multiple scene selections, such as sunset, fireworks, and outdoor action. These scene mode settings not only control the white balance, but the exposure settings as well.

Photograph in Varied Lighting

Photographers describe light by many names. These names often describe the effect that the light has on the resulting photo. Harsh light creates shadows with well-defined edges. Soft light (also called diffused light) creates shadows with soft edges. Understanding the effect that each type of light produces helps you use both types of light, and variations in between, effectively. In addition to types of lighting, the direction that the light is coming from also affects how accurately the automatic light meter can read the scene and produce optimum exposure settings.

Hard Light

Hard bright light creates a concentrated spotlight effect. Hard light from the bright sun, a flash, or a bare light bulb creates shadows with sharp edges, and obliterates highlight and shadow details. Hard light (also called direct sunlight) is good for landscape and especially for fall color photography. But you should avoid photographing people in hard light, if you can. To prevent shadows on faces caused by hard light, use a fill flash, or if possible, move the subject to a shady area.

Soft Light

Soft light is diffused light that is spread over a larger area. Atmospheric conditions, such as clouds, diffuse natural light, creating shadow edges that transition gradually. Soft light works well for portraits and close-up photography. Even though an overcast day produces a bluish color cast, the diffused light it offers allows you to get photos of subjects without harsh shadows.

Front Lighting

Front lighting strikes the subject straight on. This type of lighting can produce a flat, one-dimensional effect. If shooting with a flash, make sure the background is far enough behind the subject to prevent a cast shadow on the wall or door behind them. If you have an external flash with an adjustable head, you should try bouncing the flash off the ceiling to create a softer light.

Side Lighting

Side lighting places the light to the side of and at the same height as the subject. This lighting shows one side of the subject brightly lit, and the other side in deep shadow. Side lighting works well for rugged, angular portraits of men, but many consider it too harsh for portraits of women.

Top Lighting

Top lighting illuminates the subject from overhead, such as what happens at noon on a sunny, cloudless day. This lighting produces strong, deep shadows, especially under the eyes, nose, and chin. Although this lighting direction works for some subjects, for other subjects, you can use fill flash to add light to the shadow areas, as shown.

Back Lighting

Light positioned behind the subject creates a condition called backlighting. This typically happens when someone is standing in a dark area with a brightly lit background. This type of light confuses light meters and the subject becomes a silhouette. Depending on the angle, it can also display a thin halo of light that outlines the shape of the subject. If you do not want the subject to be shown as a silhouette, you can use the fill flash option on your camera.

Use a Flash

The electronic flash is a powerful, automatic tool. When you need to add light in a low-light scene, the camera automatically fires the flash to provide enough light for a good exposure. When a light source is producing shadows on a subject's face, using the camera's built-in flash unit or an external unit removes the shadows and creates a well illuminated photograph.

Flash Distance

To get the best flash pictures, indoors or outdoors, it is important to know the distance that the flash travels, and then to stay within that distance when taking pictures. On most compact cameras, the flash range is 10 to 15 feet. Be sure to check your camera manual to find the exact range of your flash.

Flash Compensation

Some digital cameras and accessory flash units allow you to control the flash intensity. You can set the flash to different levels of power that are measured in Exposure Values (EV). To decrease the flash output and create a softer light, you can set it to a negative EV value. Today's digital cameras automatically sense when the flash has produced the optimum exposure and adjust the flash duration. Your camera does this by using a sensor on the camera body. Learn where your camera's flash sensor is from the manual and make sure that you do not accidentally cover it with your finger when taking flash photos.

Use Flash Outdoors

You can use your camera's built-in flash outdoors to add light to pictures of people and still life subjects that are at least 5 feet away. Using a flash in overcast and shady scenes often adds noticeable color and increased contrast to images. Here, fill flash increased the color and brightness of a crate of apples and brought out details of the apples in the shadows.

Without Fill Flash

Harsh overhead (top) lighting and backlighting create problems, such as unattractive shadows in portraits and silhouettes. In this picture, without a fill flash, deep shadows appear under the nose and chin of the subject.

With Fill Flash

Depending on the make of the camera, the name used for the fill flash setting might be called "manual." In most cameras today, just opening the flash or changing the flash mode to manual will produce the necessary flash exposure to work as an effective fill flash. Even though the flash mode may be called "manual," the automatic sensor still regulates the amount of power in the flash. In this picture, fill flash lightens the deep shadow areas by adding light to the front of the subject.

Controlling Exposure and Focal Length

There are many settings that affect your digital camera photographs. Most of these settings are controlled automatically by the camera in response to the amount of light illuminating your subject and the distance of the subject from you. From aperture to shutter speed to focal length, you can mix and match different camera settings to gain creative control over your pictures. All you need is an understanding of the basic elements of photography.

The sensitivity of film to light is described as the speed of the film. Film that is very sensitive is called fast film and can take photos in lower lighting conditions than can be achieved with slower speed film. Similar to film speeds, the ISO settings on digital cameras indicate the digital image sensor's speed, or sensitivity to light. The numbers on the camera's ISO approximate the sensitivity of the same ISO number on film.

ISO stands for International Standards Organization, which created a standard measurement for the film speed of color negative and positive (slide) film. The name ISO replaced ASA (American Standard Association) in 1974, but the measurement system was the same.

ISO Settings

Although most digital cameras control the ISO setting automatically, on some digital cameras, you can set the ISO either from a dial or from the camera menu. Some digital cameras allow you to increase the ISO to very high numbers. Choosing a faster or higher ISO allows you to take pictures in scenes with less light without a flash, as shown. The drawback to using high ISO settings is that it can result in increased *noise,* small multicolor flecks, in the picture. For well-lit scenes, the lowest ISO setting (usually 125 or 200) works well.

The camera aperture, controlled by a diaphragm mechanism, determines how much or how little the lens opens to let in the light that strikes the image sensor. The size of the aperture also affects how much of the image is in focus.

Set the F-Stop

Aperture is shown as f-stop numbers, such as f/2.8, f/4, f/5.6, and f/8. These numbers refer to whether the diaphragm mechanism opens a little or a lot. A wide f-stop, such as f/2.8, allows more light to strike the image sensor. A narrow f-stop, such as f/16, lets in less light. Lenses that offer larger apertures are referred to as fast. They tend to be physically larger and more expensive than the same focal length offering a smaller aperture.

Set the Aperture

The default mode for most digital cameras is to automatically set the aperture. If the camera is set to aperture-priority mode, then you can control the aperture by choosing the f-stop on one of the camera's menus. The camera automatically sets the correct shutter speed. In manual mode, you choose the aperture and the shutter speed.

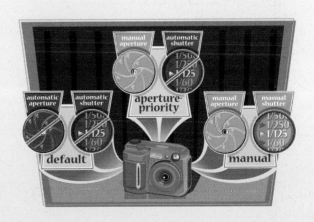

Control Depth of Field

When the automatic focus mechanism of your digital camera focuses on a subject, you can only be sure that the subject is in focus. Objects closer to and farther from the camera may not be in focus. What is in focus is controlled by the *depth of field*, which refers to the area in front of and behind a subject that is in acceptably sharp focus. In general, the zone of sharpness extends one-third in front of and two-thirds behind the point you focus on.

Pictures with a soft background show little depth of field, achieved by setting a wide aperture such as f/4, moving closer to the subject, or selecting portrait mode, if your camera offers it. Pictures with the foreground and much of the background in focus show extensive depth of field, achieved by setting a narrow aperture, such as f/11, moving farther from the subject, or selecting a landscape mode, if the subject is far enough away.

Adjust the Aperture

To increase the depth of field in a photo where you want as much of the scene in sharp focus as possible, choose a narrow aperture such as f/8 or f/11. A quick way to reduce the aperture size is to zoom out the lens. As the lens is zoomed toward telephoto, it reduces the aperture. To decrease the depth of field in a photo where you want the background to be out of focus, choose a Portrait mode or select a wider aperture such as f/2.8, f/4, or f/5.6.

Change the Camera-to-Subject Distance

Regardless of the f-stop you choose, the farther away you are from a subject, the greater the depth of field. As you move closer to a subject, the zone of acceptable focus, or depth of field, narrows.

Change Lens Focal Length

Focal length determines how much of a scene the lens *sees*. A wide-angle lens or zoom setting sees more of the scene than a telephoto lens or zoom setting. A wide-angle lens or zoom setting provides greater depth of field than a telephoto lens or zoom setting, if you are not extremely close to the subject.

Shutter speed controls how long the *curtain*, a mechanism that covers the sensor, stays open to let light from the lens strike the image sensor. The longer the shutter stays open, the more light reaches the sensor, at the aperture you set.

Shutter speeds are described by how long they allow light into cameras in fractions of a second. They range from slow, 1 second, 1/2, 1/4, 1/8, 1/15, 1/30, 1/60 sec., to fast, 1/125, 1/500, 1/1000 sec. Increasing or decreasing the shutter speed by one setting halves or doubles the exposure respectively.

Set the Shutter Speed

On fully automatic cameras, or in a program or scene mode on other cameras, the camera sets the shutter speed. For example, in Sports scene mode, the camera selects a fast shutter speed to freeze subject motion. In semi-automatic modes, you can set the shutter speed using one of the camera's menus.

Freeze or Blur Subject Motion

To freeze motion in normal scenes, set the shutter speed to 1/60 sec. or faster. To capture motion as a blur, use 1/30 sec. or slower, and mount the camera on a tripod. At a slow shutter speed, such as 1/30 sec., you can follow subject movement with the camera and blur the background, as shown here. This technique is called a *pan-blur*.

Discover Exposure Modes

Digital cameras offer several ways to control the exposure settings. Ranging from fully automatic (known also as point-and-shoot) preset scene modes, to specific exposure modes, each method of control offers advantages and disadvantages. Although serious photo buffs will eschew the automatic settings, on average, they offer the greatest insurance for getting a good photo. Selecting a preset scene mode or an exposure mode gives you greater, more creative control over depth of field and whether you freeze or blur motion.

Auto Mode

Auto mode, sometimes called program mode, works well when you want to just point and shoot. In this mode, the camera selects the aperture, or f-stop, and shutter speed for the correct exposure. Although auto mode may not be the most creative way to use your camera, it works well when your goal is to quickly capture a picture.

Aperture-Priority Mode

You can use aperture-priority mode when you want to choose the aperture, or f-stop, and have the camera automatically set the shutter speed. Aperture-priority mode works well when you want creative control over depth of field. If you choose a narrow f-stop in a low-light scene, you may need to steady the camera on a tripod due to the slow shutter speed.

Shutter-Priority Mode

You can use shutter-priority mode when you want to choose the shutter speed and have the camera automatically set the correct aperture, or f-stop. Shutter-priority mode works well when you want to control how action appears. A fast shutter speed freezes action. A slow shutter speed shows motion as a blur, as shown.

Subject Modes

You can use a subject or scene mode when you want the camera to automatically set the exposure based on a specific scene. Common scene modes include sports, landscape, portrait, and close-up. Newer cameras offer special modes such as sunsets, fireworks, or sunrise. Scene modes work well when you want to point and shoot and use classic exposure settings that are appropriate to the scene, such as the early morning shot shown.

Manual Mode

You can use manual mode when you want to choose the shutter speed and the aperture. Manual mode works well when you want control over depth of field and the ability to freeze or blur motion. When you change the f-stop or the shutter speed, the camera shows the appropriate setting for the other variable in the viewfinder. Consult your camera manual for specific instructions.

Learn About Focal Length

Focal length determines the angle of view, or how much of a scene the camera's lens sees. In addition, focal length plays a role in determining the sharpness or softness of the background and foreground objects in a scene, or the depth of field.

To learn more about depth of field, see the section "Control Depth of Field," earlier in this chapter.

Focal Length Defined

Focal length describes how much of the scene the lens sees, or the angle of view of the lens. For example, on a 35mm camera, a 17mm lens has a wider angle of view than the human eye can see, encompassing a broad sweep of the scene. A telephoto lens has a much narrower view, and focuses on a single, distant element.

Use a Normal Lens

On a 35mm camera, a 50mm to 55mm lens is considered a normal lens because it sees approximately the same angle of view as the human eye sees. On most digital cameras, a 35mm lens is closer to normal because the image sensor is smaller than the traditional 35mm film frame, which magnifies the view approximately 1.5 times depending on the camera sensor. This is why all digital camera makers list the focal length as being "equivalent" to a specific 35mm focal length. This is helpful for traditional film photographers as focal length is a term they understand.

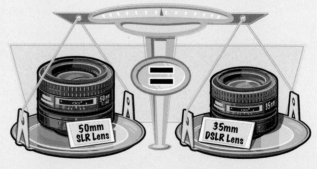

A wide-angle, or wider than 50mm, lens provides a broad angle of view and extensive depth of field — especially at small apertures, if you are not standing close to the subject. Use a wide-angle lens or zoom setting to photograph landscapes, panoramas, large groups, and small areas where you want to capture the entire scene.

Wide-Angle Distortion

Wide-angle lenses distort the relative size and spacing of objects in a scene. For example, objects close to the lens seem larger than they are, while distant objects seem farther away, and farther apart than you remember seeing them. A wide-angle lens, or a zoom lens at its widest setting, creates a distortion called *barrel distortion*, which is evident in the buildings on the edges bending inward, as shown.

Aspherical Lens

An aspherical lens has a nonspherical surface. These lenses help correct optical flaws to produce better edge sharpness and straighter lines. These lenses are also lighter in weight than nonaspherical lenses because they do not need additional lens elements, or additional glass, to correct for edge sharpness.

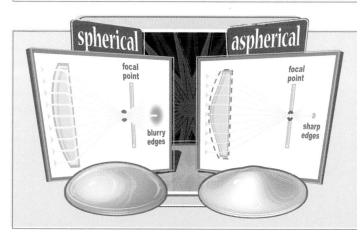

Use a Telephoto Lens

A telephoto, or wider than 50mm, lens provides a narrow angle of view and limited depth of field. You can use a telephoto lens or zoom setting to isolate a subject from the background, bring distant objects closer, and compress objects with the background.

Telephoto Compression

Because telephoto lenses compress perspective, elements in a scene appear closer together than you remember seeing them. You can use this compression to create a layering effect in photos.

Low-Dispersion Glass

Telephoto lenses and zooms with low-dispersion glass provide increased sharpness, especially at the frame edges, and they provide better color. When you shop for a compact camera or a telephoto lens, look for lenses identified as ED, extra-low dispersion; LD, low dispersion; SLD, super-low dispersion; L, luxury; or APO, apochromatic.

All digital cameras that are not SLR cameras have a built-in zoom lens. A zoom lens enables you to change the focal length of the camera at the touch of a button. A zoom lens combines a range of focal distances within a single lens. Zoom lenses fall within the standard lens categories of wide-angle, for 17mm to 35mm, and telephoto, for 80mm to 200mm.

Choose a Zoom Lens

When you shop for a digital camera, make sure that it has an optical zoom lens. In addition to this, you should get as large of a zoom factor as possible. The trade-off of having a large zoom factor is that the camera is typically larger and a little bulky. The advantage is the ability to zoom in, allowing you to capture details at a distance that would otherwise not be possible. Without a hefty zoom, it would not be possible to photograph shy creatures, such as the bird shown.

Prevent Blurry Pictures

Zooming in on your subject exaggerates even the slightest camera movement, resulting in blurred images, especially when you take photos at slower shutter speeds. When shooting at slower shutter speeds, you can stabilize your camera by mounting it on a tripod. Some newer cameras now offer a built-in vibration reduction that reduces (but does not remove) the effects of lens shake.

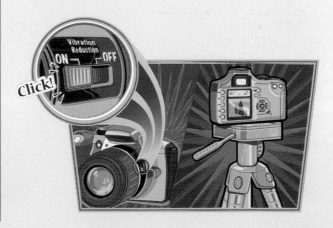

Understanding a Multiplication Factor

Digital cameras with image sensors smaller than a 35mm film frame reduce the angle of view and produce an apparent lens magnification. Magnification varies by factors ranging from 1.3 to 1.5 times. At a 1.5 factor, a 100mm to 300mm lens provides a 150mm to 450mm equivalent angle of view. This gives greater magnification when you photograph distant subjects, but gives a narrower view of the scene at wide-angle settings.

Optical Versus Digital Zoom

Many digital cameras offer optical and digital zoom. Optical zoom magnifies the scene by changing the focal length. Digital zoom crops the scene and then magnifies the center of the frame to make the subject appear larger. Some cameras add extra pixels to round out the image size or resolution. This cropping effect often degrades image quality. Always avoid using digital zoom.

Digital-Specific Lenses

Because the size of the sensor in a digital camera is physically smaller than a 35mm negative, professional digital SLR cameras make larger and much more expensive sensors. A sensor that is the same size as a 35mm negative is called full frame. Companies including Olympus, Kodak, and Fujifilm promote the *four-thirds system* that establishes a new common standard for the interchange of lenses developed for digital SLR cameras. The four-thirds system allows the development of dedicated digital-camera lens systems with a sensor measuring only half the size of a 35mm film frame. The four-thirds system produces a 2× multiplier for the new digital lenses.

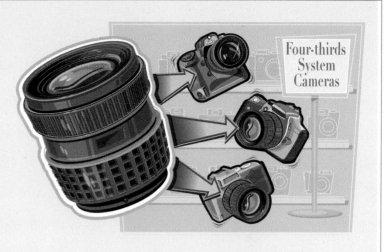

Four-thirds System Cameras

viewfinder

lens view

What You See Versus What the Lens Sees

Many compact digital cameras feature optical viewfinders, but the viewfinders are separate from the lens. As a result, you do not see in the viewfinder exactly what the lens sees. The closer you move to the subject, the greater the difference, or *parallax*, becomes. To get an accurate view of what the lens *sees*, you should use the LCD. Viewing the image on the LCD can be tricky on a bright sunny day. There are accessories that put a hood over the LCD to allow you to see the LCD on the brightest of days.

Learning About Focus

Focus is essential to taking good photographs. If the subject is blurry or not in focus, it makes the picture unusable. Even though all digital cameras have an autofocusing system, focus problems are the leading cause of ruined photos in digital photography. In this chapter, you learn how to focus precisely, and what to focus on in a scene.

Understanding Focus Systems

All digital cameras have autofocus built in. These systems vary from camera to camera and their abilities range from a simple type of autofocus that focuses the camera on the subject in the center of the frame to more sophisticated systems that can follow and focus on objects moving across the lens or set to focus on one subject at the exclusion of everything else in the scene.

With a little understanding about how the autofocus system on your camera works, you can ensure that your photos are consistently in focus.

Fixed Focus Systems

Fixed focus systems do not adjust the lens to focus, but rely only on having such a great depth of field that everything more than a few feet in front of the camera is in focus. Although the method is simple, fixed focus systems often display only reasonably sharp pictures. Budget film cameras and single-use film cameras often use a fixed focus system.

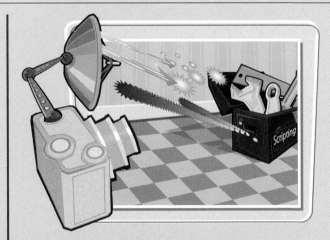

Active Autofocus Systems

Many cameras use an active system that uses a short burst of light or infrared to determine distance. These systems measure the amount of time it takes for the light to be reflected back to the camera by an object, and use this distance to set the focus. Active systems can be fast and precise, but often have problems with shooting through windows and other glass surfaces.

Passive Autofocus Systems

Some cameras use passive autofocus systems, also called *phase detection*. To determine camera-to-subject distance, the camera detects differences in dark and light elements, or *contrast*, in the scene, or differences in colors and textures. Passive autofocus works well in normal contrast scenes, but does not focus as well in low-light scenes and with subjects that have little contrast difference (for example, a solid blank wall). Passive autofocus systems sometimes get confused as to focus subjects. In the picture, even though the car in the center is the subject, the autofocus system chose to focus on the object closest to the camera,, which is the flower on the right.

Multipoint Autofocus Systems

Multipoint autofocus systems let you easily compose with and focus on an off-center subject. To focus, you select one of the autofocus sensors, place the subject within the selected sensor, and then focus by pressing the Shutter Release button halfway down. Some multipoint systems offer focus tracking to maintain continuous focus on a moving subject while others focus on the closest subject regardless of where it is in the frame.

When Autofocus Fails

Autofocus does not always focus correctly. The most common cause of failure is the camera focusing on the wrong subject. The next most common cause of failure is when there is too little light on the subject, as shown in this picture. Most cameras have an indicator (a small icon or a beep) that lets you know when the camera thinks it is in focus. After you take the photo, you can see it in the camera's LCD screen, but be aware that even blurred images can appear sharp when viewed on a tiny LCD screen. For important photos, you should use the LCD's zoom feature and make sure the subject, and not the background, is in focus.

Focus on a Still Subject

When composing an image in the frame, it is desirable to have the subject off-center. But, because the autofocus system of many cameras expects the subject to be in the center, it attempts to focus on whatever is in the center of the frame. This makes focusing difficult with cameras that have a single-center autofocus sensor. To compose an image with the subject off-center, you can use focus lock.

Focus on a Still Subject

1 Frame your subject in the viewfinder or LCD.

Always set the zoom before focusing.

For multipoint focusing systems, choose the autofocus sensor you want.

Note: *See Chapter 4 to learn about using a zoom lens.*

2 Press the Shutter Release button halfway down.

The focus system locks using the center autofocus sensor or the sensor you chose.

3 Check the focus indicator on the camera to ensure the focus is good.

Most cameras have a green LED that glows in or near the viewfinder when the subject is in focus.

④ Continue to hold the button halfway down while shifting the camera to recompose the scene.

⑤ Fully depress the Shutter Release button to take the picture.

Note: If you or the subject changes position, be sure to repeat this process to refocus on the subject.

The camera captures the properly focused picture and saves it to memory.

Should I compose my pictures using the viewfinder or the LCD?

The LCD provides an accurate view of the scene that the camera captures, whereas the viewfinder may not show the full scene. If you use the LCD to compose pictures, be sure that the focus indicator shows that the focus is good before you take the picture. When you compose using the LCD in low lighting conditions, consider supporting the camera on a solid surface such as a tripod or a table, or brace yourself against a solid object to ensure that you get sharp pictures.

Use Focus Modes

One of the features that is becoming popular with digital cameras is the ability to select a preset mode. Several cameras offer as many as ten of these presets. Selecting some of these subject or scene modes affects the focus method used. You can read the camera manual to discover which of the modes affect focus and how they affect it.

Automatic

Automatic is usually the default setting of the camera. It does not affect the autofocus system and allows you to take photos at distances from a few feet to infinity.

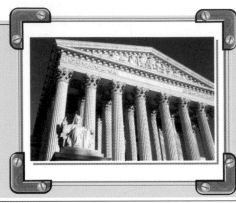

Landscape

If you set the camera to landscape scene mode, then the camera turns off autofocus and sets the focus at infinity. The advantage of this mode is that it prevents the camera from continually attempting to focus on a subject that is too far away, which takes time and battery. Because landscape scene mode disables autofocus, the only caution when using this mode is to remember to return the mode to normal auto after you take the photo.

Close-Up or Macro

To change the focus for closer distances, switch to close-up or macro mode. Depending on your camera, switching to macro mode allows the focusing system to focus on subjects as close as .8 inches from the front of the lens. Check your camera manual to see what the minimum and maximum focus distance is for macro mode. In many cameras, the maximum distance for macro is around 30 feet, which also makes it good for portraits.

Discover Focus Techniques

Focus on a Moving Subject

Moving subjects can be a challenge because most camera autofocus systems do not focus quickly. One way to ensure that the subject is in the frame when the photo is taken is to establish the focus before you shoot using focus lock. This way the camera is prefocused and will not waste time hunting for the correct focus. The other way is to set the camera to continuous, and then press the button and hold it down. You end up with multiple images to choose from and the odds are that one of them will be great.

Choose a Point of Focus

When taking a portrait or group picture, focus on the eyes of the person who is closest to the camera. When photographing a still life, focus on the most important element in the scene. For example, in this picture, the focus is on the food on the plate, not the wine or the background. For a landscape photo, fix the focus one-third of the way into the scene.

Focus Tips

- Use a tripod if the lighting is low (see Chapter 2).
- Be sure your focus indicator shows that your camera is in focus.
- Use your camera's LCD screen to review the photo to make sure it is in focus.
- For important images, zoom in the LCD preview to make sure the focus is sharp because even blurry images can appear sharp on a small LCD screen.

Focus Tips:
1. Use a Tripod
2. Check Focus
3. Use LCD
4. Use Zoom In or

6

Composing Pictures Like a Pro

Want to quickly improve your digital pictures? Improving composition is a quick way to get better pictures. This chapter explores some simple techniques used by professional photographers that will immediately improve the photos that you take. You also learn ways to add interest to all your photos using a variety of composition techniques.

The best pictures not only catch your attention, but they also hold your attention. To get these kinds of pictures, compose images carefully and tell a story in each picture. Begin by borrowing established design principles and composition techniques that artists and photographers have been using since the camera was invented. As you progress, add in your own personal style to create signature pictures that viewers remember.

Stand Back and Evaluate

You interpret each scene for your viewers. It is your job to combine your emotional perceptions with the objective viewpoint of the camera. Begin by evaluating all the elements in the scene. Gradually narrow your view to identify individual vignettes. Then look for defining elements, colors, patterns, and textures that can help organize the visual information in the picture.

Consider Audience and Occasion

The most important questions to ask during this stage are, "Why am I taking this picture?" and "What do I want to tell the viewer?" Answering these questions helps you focus on the important elements in the scene. From there, you can choose to include or exclude visual elements that add to or detract from the message you want to communicate to viewers.

Use Light and Exposure Controls Creatively

When you know the message you want to convey, you can use or modify the light, and choose exposure settings that create the mood, concentrate attention, and provide the perspective of the scene. In this picture, having the young woman stand in the shade gives her image a hint of mystery. To learn more about light, see Chapter 3. To learn more about exposure, see Chapter 4.

Keep It Simple

Just as with writing or painting, messages are most effectively delivered and retained when they are simple. Strive for a clean shot — an uncluttered visual scene that conveys a single story, or conveys a clear graphic shape, as shown here. To get a clean shot, you can clear away clutter, change your shooting position, or zoom in on the subject.

Evaluate the Result

With a digital camera, you can immediately evaluate the success or failure of your images on the LCD. Take advantage of the opportunity to make adjustments, and immediately reshoot the picture. The more pictures that you take, review, and reshoot, the better you become at recognizing composition problems by looking at pictures on the LCD.

Consider Design Principles

Many principles of photographic composition are derived from the traditional design disciplines of art and graphic design, some of which date back to the Renaissance. Here are a few of the most widely used principles.

How the Shapes of Objects Affect Photos

The number and kind of shapes in a photo determine where viewers focus their attention. The human shape or form always draws attention in a picture. A single, small shape attracts attention either as the subject or as a secondary element that helps define the subject. Groupings of similar objects invite the viewer to compare size, shape, and spacing between the objects.

Create a Sense of Balance

Balance is a sense of "rightness" in a photo. A balanced photo does not appear to be too heavy at any point, or too off-center. When composing your pictures, consider the following: the visual weight of colors and tones — dark is heavier than light; objects — large objects appear heavier than light objects; and placement — objects placed toward an edge appear heavier than objects placed at the center of the frame.

What Lines Convey

Lines have symbolic significance that you can use to direct the focus and organize the visual elements in your picture. Horizontal lines imply stability and peacefulness. Diagonal lines imply strength, as shown in this picture, and dynamic tension. Vertical lines imply motion, while curved lines symbolize grace, and zigzag lines imply action.

Is Symmetry Good or Bad?

Perfectly symmetrical compositions, images that are the same from side to side or from top to bottom, create balance and stability, but they also are viewed as boring compositions. Symmetrical designs, as shown here, often offer less visual impact than photos with some asymmetry and tension.

Placement of a Subject within a Picture

Just as symmetry is visually uninteresting, placing a subject or the line of the horizon in the center of the frame is usually equally boring. Subject placement depends on the scene, but placement should identify the subject and create a natural visual path through the photo. Also, motion and implied action should come into the frame rather than travel out of it.

Discover Rules of Composition

There are many established rules and guidelines that you can use to improve your photos. Most of them are simple and easy to remember. There are no binding rules of composition. Some of the greatest artists today broke the rules of composition and technique of their time. The techniques in this section provide a good starting point for designing images. Be sure to experiment and let the subject help define your composition.

"Society honors its live conformists and its dead nonconformists." – Mark Twain

Practice the Rule of Thirds

A popular photography compositional technique draws an imaginary grid over the viewfinder. With the scene divided into thirds, the photographer places the subject on one of the points of intersection or along one of the lines on the grid. In a portrait, you can place the eyes of the subject at the upper-left intersection point, which is considered to be the strongest position.

Frame the Subject

Photographers often borrow a technique from painters, putting the subject within a naturally occurring frame, such as a tree framed by a barn door, or a distant building framed by an archway in the foreground, as shown. The frame may or may not be in focus, but for it to be most effective, it should add context to the subject.

Fill the Frame

Just as an artist fills an entire canvas with a scene, photographers strive to fill the image frame with elements that support the message. Decide exactly what you want in the picture, and then fill the frame with what you choose for the picture. For variation, you can come in very close to the subject to show only part of the subject.

Use Other Composition Aids

Other composition techniques include using strong textures, repeating patterns and geometric shapes, and color repetition or contrasts to compose images. These elements can create a picture on their own, or you can use them to create visual motion that directs the eye or supports the subject.

Choose the Orientation

The most basic composition begins by choosing either a horizontal or a vertical orientation. Some subjects dictate the most appropriate orientation. For example, you can use a horizontal orientation for a sweeping landscape, and a vertical orientation for a portrait, as shown in this picture. Otherwise, choose the orientation that supports the composition you envision and avoids useless, empty space.

Check the Background and Surroundings

In a picture, the elements behind and around the subject become as much a part of the photograph as the subject, as shown in the photo of the young lady from Texas. As you compose the picture, check everything in the viewfinder or LCD for objects that compete with or distract from the subject. Then see if you can move the objects, the subject, or change your position to eliminate distractions.

Learn to Control Composition

In a perfect world, you could control all the elements within a photograph. In a studio, everything is controlled by the photographer. In the outside world, you must work with existing conditions, backgrounds, and foregrounds. Here are some ways to get the best composition when you cannot control all the elements in the scene.

Select Focus and Control Depth of Field

Because the eye is drawn to the sharpest part of the photo, you can use focus to emphasize the relative importance of elements in the picture. Or combine selective focus and depth of field to emphasize or subdue elements within the picture. Here, a shallow depth of field blurs a distracting background. For more information on depth of field, see Chapter 4.

Change the Point of View

Instead of photographing at eye level, try changing your viewpoint. For instance, if you photograph a subject from a lower-than-eye-level position, then the subject seems powerful, while a higher-than-eye-level position creates the opposite effect.

Use Tone and Contrast

You can use *contrast,* or the difference between light and dark tones, to emphasize your subject. Experiment by modifying the amount and angle of light to create more or less contrast, such as waiting for the sun to be in a position to produce long shadows, as shown. Or you can change position so the subject is backlit to add dramatic contrast.

Define Space and Perspective

Some techniques to control the perception of space in pictures include changing the distance from the camera to the subject, selecting a telephoto or wide-angle lens or zoom setting, changing the position of the light, and changing the point of view. In this example, a telephoto lens compresses the dry grasses blowing in the wind.

Putting It All Together

In this chapter, you can practice and see the results of using different exposure factors, lenses or zoom settings, lighting, and scene modes.

Experiment with Depth of Field

Learning to control depth of field (DOF) in a picture gives you the ability to choose what part of the scene is in focus and what part is blurred. You can also control the amount of blurring; from mild softness to unrecognizable blurs. You can use depth of field to guide the attention of the viewer and to create artistic effects.

Control Viewer Focus

There are several ways to control depth of field. The easiest way, if your camera has one, is to select its portrait or macro scene mode. The portrait mode preset on your camera should not be confused with the term describing the orientation of the photo as in portrait and landscape. The portrait mode sets the camera to use the widest possible aperture to shorten the depth of field. The macro mode also produces a short depth of field because the subject is so close to the lens. You can also use aperture, focal length, and camera-to-subject distance, individually or in combination, to control depth of field. Other than scene mode, increasing the aperture (using a smaller f-stop) or getting closer to the subject is the next best way to decrease depth of field in a photo. Be aware that you cannot see the blur effect when composing the image, only after you have taken the photo and are reviewing it in the LCD.

Limits to Control

Sometimes you cannot use the aperture you want because the scene is too bright. In this picture, the bright afternoon sunlight did not allow the use of a wide aperture to limit depth of field. Because the pumpkins have shiny skins, putting a polarizer filter on the camera reduces the sun reflections on the pumpkins and also reduces the amount of light coming into the lens allowing use of a larger aperture. The result is a decreased depth of field, singling out the pumpkin from the background.

Get the Effect You Want

The pictures on this page show how narrow, mid-range, and wide apertures affect depth of field, or the zone of sharpness from front to back, in a picture. In this picture, taken in a New Orleans cemetery, the zoom was used at its widest setting and because it was a bright sunny day, the aperture was small (f/22), creating a wide depth of field that allowed both the closest and the farthest mausoleums to be in focus.

Focus on the Subject

In this picture, the scene mode of the camera was set to portrait. This scene mode causes your camera to produce a short depth of field so you have a soft, blurred background. Because the family members in the portrait are not all the same distance from the camera, the father at the back of the photo is slightly out of focus. This can be prevented by using the zoom feature of your LCD preview and soft checking that all the subjects are in focus before you leave the photo shoot.

Classic Landscape and Portrait Apertures

A general rule of photography has been as follows: For landscape pictures, use a narrow aperture to create extensive depth of field. For portraits, use a wide aperture to decrease depth of field. Today's cameras generally do this for you automatically. Using the portrait mode changes the camera settings to produce a narrow depth of field. Most cameras also have a landscape scene mode that turns off autofocus and sets the focus to infinity, producing the greatest depth of field possible. It usually is not necessary to use this mode, because the camera's autofocus mechanism detects the range and changes the focus to infinity. The photo shown was taken using a camera that was in normal autofocus mode and it still produced maximum depth of field.

Now that you know how depth of field affects pictures, you can apply this knowledge to create different specific effects or to find an acceptable exposure in difficult scenes.

Maximize Overall Sharpness

For maximum detail from front to back in a picture, use the widest setting of your camera's zoom lens that still allows you to keep the composition you envisioned. Next, if your camera allows it, change the aperture to the narrowest setting (largest number). As you decrease the aperture size, you notice that the camera automatically changes the shutter speed to compensate for less light coming through the lens. Do not let the shutter speed drop below 1/60 sec. Below that speed, the camera movement or the movement of the subject will blur the photograph. For the sharpest possible photo, try stabilizing the camera by setting it on a fence post or a railing.

Maximize Sharpness Up-Close

You can use the macro scene mode of the camera, and a close camera-to-subject distance to get acceptable sharpness up-close. The macro setting of most digital cameras works within a fixed range of the zoom lens setting. Read your manual to find out how the macro setting works on your model. Be aware that most macro settings have a very narrow depth of field. As shown, both the front and back of a small flower can be out of focus. The only way to ensure that the entire subject is in focus is to carefully review the image in the LCD after shooting a few test shots.

Get a Limited Area of Sharpness

You can combine a telephoto lens, a wider aperture, and a closer camera-to-subject distance for the ideal portrait setting. To emphasize a detail of the subject, move closer to the subject. If your subject is a person, consider whether sharp detail in your photo is cute or undesirable. In the photo shown, the result is cute. The same detail of an older person brings out wrinkles and other effects of aging that are less desirable.

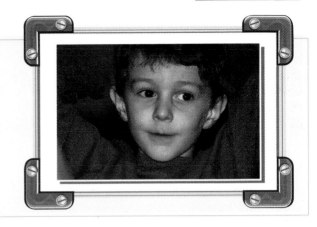

Get Maximum Sharpness in Extreme Close-Ups

If your camera does not have a dedicated macro scene mode, you can combine a telephoto lens, a narrow aperture, and a close camera-to-subject distance when you want to photograph close-up, or *macro*, photos. Because the working distance is close, you can get better depth of field by choosing a narrow aperture. All these things combine to reduce the amount of light entering the camera. When shooting a photo of African beads on a bright sunny day, as shown, this works well. When shooting a photo in early morning or late afternoon light, the reduced light may affect the autofocus, making it necessary to use manual focus. To compensate for the reduced light, the camera will reduce the shutter speed, so be sure to use a tripod to ensure a sharp picture.

Get Sharp, Everyday Pictures

The key for getting sharp everyday photos is to ensure that the camera is set to the right mode, that the autofocus indicator shows the subject is in focus, and that the camera is focused on the subject of the image and not something else in the frame. For everyday shooting, use the auto settings and you will usually get great results with good sharpness.

Change Shutter Speed for Effect

The shutter speed on most digital cameras ranges from shutter times of several seconds to one or two thousandths of a second. Your camera automatically selects the optimum shutter speed based on the available light in the scene. You can select different shutter speeds to stop action or to show action or motion as a blur. You can also experiment with shutter speeds to create unexpected and interesting results.

Stop the Action

You can stop action at shutter speeds faster than 1/125 sec. Faster shutter speeds work well for capturing an athlete in mid-air, or for showing subtle action such as a spinning top that looks as if it is standing still. The problem with freezing images using high shutter speeds is that it loses its feeling of motion. The photo of the Second World War–era bomber appears to be hanging in space with its propellers stationary and does not look like it is flying at several hundred miles per hour.

Show the Action

At 1/30 sec. and slower shutter speeds, you can show action as a blur, as in this picture of a slow-moving waterfall. Had a faster shutter speed been used, the water would have appeared frozen. By using a slower shutter speed, it is possible to capture the sense of the water flowing in the creek. Slow shutter speeds are also used to capture light trails created by passing traffic at dusk, or for creative light compositions.

You can use focus as a way to direct the attention of the viewer to the most important or a single element in a picture. In close-ups, you can switch to manual focus to get the best focus.

Combine Selective Focus with Distance

To show a small area with fine detail, use a selective focus. In this picture, a narrow aperture of f/32 and sharp focus emphasize the fine details of the flowers on the right. In macro pictures, you can switch to manual focus to ensure the sharpest focus.

Combine Selective Focus, Focal Length, and Aperture

When you combine a wide aperture setting with a telephoto lens, and focus carefully, you can narrow the focus even more. As shown in this picture, a telephoto lens and an aperture of f/4.5 create a very specific focus.

Compose Creatively

You cannot use all these techniques every time you take a photo. As you practice the techniques in this book over and over again, they will become second nature to you. You will get a feel for not only how but when to use them. At that point you can combine exposure, focal length, and composition to take creative pictures that convey a message or tell a story.

Get to the Point

In this image, the focus of the composition was not on the teenage girl but on the hardware she was wearing. By using a wide aperture and the zoom lens pushed out toward the telephoto end, it was possible to isolate the hardware and blur the background at the same time.

Draw the Viewer In

Here the composition guides the viewer through the flowers toward the subject, which is an old headstone. A narrow aperture creates good detail throughout the flowers to the headstone, despite the close camera-to-subject distance.

Capture the Action

In this image, a wide aperture was used and the narrow depth of field makes some of the parts of the flower appear blurred, imparting a sense of motion.

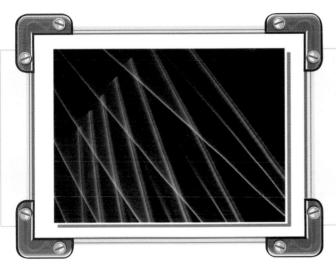

Create Abstract Images

Green neon tubes in a dark room combined with a slow shutter speed produce a unique abstract image when the camera is panned from side to side. It takes some experimentation. For this photo, the camera automatically set the shutter speed to a setting of two seconds. The camera was steadied on a table as it was rotated to prevent up and down movement.

Motion Is Good

To show the power of motion, you can combine a high shutter speed and wide aperture, as shown here. The result is a narrow depth of field that makes the foreground water and the background out of focus but leaves the mallard in sharp focus and the water frozen in space.

In most cases, the goal is to have sufficient lighting to produce an optimum exposure. Modifying light not only overcomes common problems in typical scenes, but it can also give pictures a dramatic flair.

Experiment with a Flash

A built-in flash provides the quickest and most convenient way to alter scene lighting. Experiment with the various synch modes, such as slow, front, and rear curtain synchronization synch modes. In the image shown, the speed of the busy breakfast crowd is captured using slow synch mode. You can use these modes to obtain good exposures at night and to create front or rear light trails of traffic in dimly lit scenes.

Use Fill Flash

Although fill flash works well for portraits, you can use fill flash for other subjects, as well. For example, you can use fill flash outdoors to highlight outdoor colors in nature pictures. For indoor still-life pictures, fill flash reduces deep shadows caused by daylight from windows.

Use a Reflector

You can use a reflector to catch natural light and reflect it back into a scene. In this picture, a gold-colored reflector adds light to the face of the subject and creates a warm glow. Experiment with the position of the reflector, but avoid adding too much light or creating hot spots on the subject. You can purchase small, collapsible reflectors at any camera store.

Wait for Flattering Light

To get the best pictures, you should wait for the best light of the day. Here, the warm light of the late afternoon sun makes a pile of mufflers in a junkyard appear to be made of gold.

Watch for the Best Light Plays

It is a good habit to always have your camera with you to capture some of the beautiful natural light plays. In this picture, a storm moves in at sunset, displaying a dramatic interaction of light and color.

After you practice using standard photography techniques, you can use other variations that can be fun and create interesting images.

Pan Using a Slow Shutter Speed

At a shutter speed of 1/30 sec. or slower, you can pan with a subject as it moves, making the background appear blurred. To do this, focus on a place where the subject will pass. When the subject enters the viewfinder, follow the subject with the camera, and then take the picture when the subject reaches the point on which you focused. To maintain a smooth blur, keep the camera in motion as you press and release the shutter.

Use Backlighting

In harsh light, you can sometimes turn the light to your advantage by using it to create silhouettes or to enhance vivid color. To enhance transparent color, take a low shooting position, and even a dead leaf becomes a blaze of color, as shown in this picture.

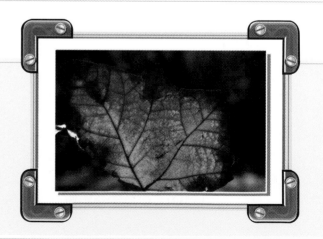

Capture Light Trails

You can create cool low-light and night images by switching to Low-Light or Night scene mode. The camera uses a slow shutter speed to capture subjects, such as moving car lights, as streaks of light. If you do not have scene modes, select a shutter speed of 1/30 sec. or slower, use a tripod, and for shutter speeds of 1 second or greater use the camera's self-timer to trip the shutter, avoiding any motion to the camera caused by touching the Shutter Release button.

Warm Up Flash Pictures

Most digital cameras compensate for the cool colors produced by the internal flash. If your flash does not correct the color imbalance, you can warm up the color of your camera flash by placing colored transparent gels or films over the flash. In the picture on the right, placing a discarded strip of photographic film over the flash adds warmth to the scene, compared to the unfiltered flash picture shown on the left.

Taking Your First Digital Photo

Learn the specifics
of setting up a digital
camera, and taking,
transferring, and
evaluating your first
set of digital pictures.

To get off to a good start with a digital camera, take time to read the manual and to set camera options to ensure that you get the best image quality. Some camera manuals are complicated, printed in several languages, and generally difficult to read. In such cases, read the quick-start guide, if available, or read the quick-start section of the user manual.

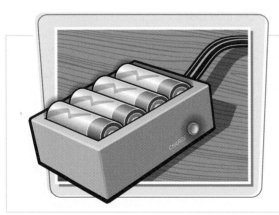

Charge Batteries

As a first step, read the instructions in the quick-start guide or the manual on charging the battery. Some batteries require an overnight charging cycle, while others charge in a few hours. Be patient and make sure the battery is fully charged before inserting the battery into the camera. While the battery is charging, you can read your manual.

Insert and Format the Memory Card

All digital cameras use a removable memory card to store images. If your memory card has a write-protect (locking) mechanism, unlock the card before inserting it into the camera. Then locate the slot for the memory card, which often includes a diagram showing the direction that you insert the card. Most cameras do not accept a memory card if inserted incorrectly, so never force it. After inserting the card, you should make a habit of formatting it, especially if you have used the card before, to remove any old photos or other digital information it may contain.

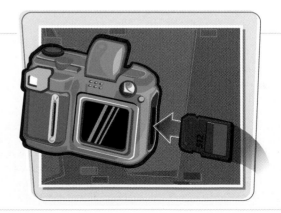

Set the Date and Time

Turn the camera on, and then set it to record or picture-taking mode. Follow the instructions on the LCD to set the date and time. You should set the date and time because they become part of the shooting information that the camera stores with images — *metadata* information that is helpful for organizing and retrieving images later. The term metadata describes a large collection of data that the camera produces and includes with each photo each time a picture is taken. In addition to time and date information, metadata includes the camera settings used during exposure, or the camera make, model, and serial number. More than 200 types of information can be included as metadata, depending on your camera.

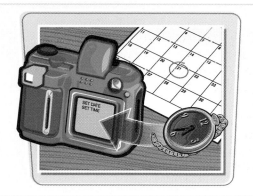

Set the Image Quality and Format

You can set image size, quality, and format on a camera menu. For best quality, set it to the largest size and highest quality. Not all cameras allow you to select the image size. The higher quality settings provide improved quality, but the images require more memory card space. Also, you can choose an image format: JPEG, TIFF, or Raw. Although TIFF is a popular format in graphics design, do not choose it for storing digital images. It takes a long time to save the images and has the same quality as the best JPEG setting. Raw, a format that stores images with no in-camera processing, provides powerful post-capture options, but you must use manufacturer or third-party software to view and save images.

Set the White Balance

Early digital cameras required you to manually set the white balance to get accurate color. Most modern cameras produce acceptable color outdoors just using the automatic settings. When doing a lot of photography under a specific type of lighting, you can set the white balance to the setting that matches the light in the scene. If you take pictures indoors under artificial light, and are not using a flash, set the white balance to the appropriate setting. If using a flash, in most cases leave the camera in its default automatic mode or whatever mode you normally use. I do not recommend changing the white balance setting to flash. If you do change the white balance to flash, make sure you change it back as soon as the flash pictures are finished or the colors in non-flash pictures will appear as if they were taken with a blue filter on the lens.

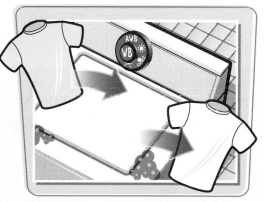

Take Test Pictures

The first pictures you take provide a great baseline for evaluating the performance and characteristics of your camera. Identifying camera characteristics tells you which camera settings to fine-tune to get consistently good pictures. In addition to identifying the camera's characteristics, it is most helpful to become familiar with the camera controls and operation.

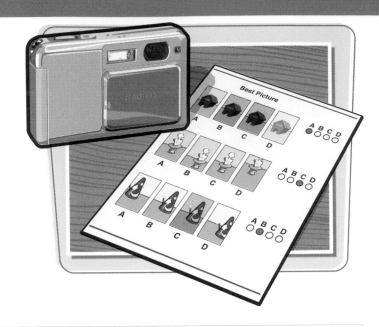

Learn the Basic Controls

Most digital cameras offer a large selection of controls, dials, buttons, and features. Begin by acquainting yourself with the basic controls used for taking and reviewing images. The controls use abbreviations and icons to indicate their function so it is helpful to learn them. Several buttons and dials are used for more than one purpose, depending on the camera mode that you select. Locate the zoom control and learn how to use it for composing images. You should also learn to review images and make selections from the camera menus.

Take Pictures

Get started by taking familiar kinds of pictures of family and friends, indoors and outdoors. Also take pictures with and without the flash, both indoors and outdoors. These pictures establish a level of comfort when using your camera, so you can take photos without having to open the manual.

Adjust to a Digital Camera

If you are accustomed to film cameras, you may need to become accustomed to slower start-up times that some cameras exhibit, and *shutter lag,* which is the delay between the time you press the shutter release button and the time the exposure is made. Image recording time depends on the size of the image file being used. Larger image files, such as Raw, take longer to save the image to the card. With the exception of large, professional digital SLR cameras, using a faster card *will not* increase how fast an image writes to the card. If the card is still writing an image to a card when you turn it off, the camera will continue to record the image until it is complete before shutting down.

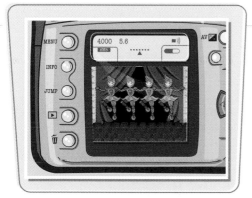

Compose Shots in the Viewfinder and LCD

For close subjects, use the LCD to compose images. *Parallax* is the slight offset between what you see in the viewfinder and what you get on the image. Parallax becomes more apparent for subjects closer than 3 feet at maximum zoom settings, and 10 feet at telephoto settings. At other distances, you can use the viewfinder to compose images.

Verify Pictures

If your camera does not have an electronic viewfinder, as you shoot, be sure to check the pictures on your LCD monitor. The LCD is too small to make definitive judgments, but it indicates obvious composition and exposure problems. Most cameras display the picture on the LCD immediately after you take it. To browse through the images, switch to a playback mode.

Error messages on a digital camera can interrupt your first photo session. However, you can solve the most common problems quickly and easily.

The Shutter Release Button Does Not Work

If the shutter release button does not work, there are several possibilities. The most common cause is that the camera's autofocus has been unable to determine the correct focus. Another less likely cause is the memory card is locked. Take out the memory card and switch the lever or tab to the unlocked position. For more about memory cards, see Chapter 2. If the card is full, the status LCD usually flashes. You need to replace it with another card or delete some images to increase the amount of room on the card.

The Camera Is On, But the Status Bar Is Blank

To conserve battery power, most cameras go into sleep mode when they are not in use for a while. You can press the main power button to wake up the camera, or you can turn the camera off and then turn it back on. Also, check to see if the memory card is full, or if the battery needs to be recharged or replaced.

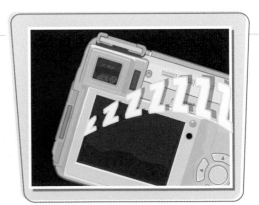

When You Cannot Save Images to an Empty Memory Card

Sometimes when a memory card is formatted by a computer using a card reader with an older operating system, the card is formatted incorrectly. It is a simple matter to correct. Simply use the camera to format the card by selecting the Format feature (usually from a menu selection).

Flash Pictures Are Too Dark or Too Light

All built-in flash units work within a range specified by the manufacturer, usually up to 15 feet. If flash pictures in the LCD look too dark, the subject may be too far away. Move closer to the subject and check the camera manual for the flash distance range. If the photo is washed out, you may be covering the flash sensor with your finger when taking the photos. A finger obstructing the flash sensor prevents it from correctly reading the flash when it fires. Check your camera manual to learn where your flash sensor is located.

Pictures Are Blurry

Digital cameras include a focus indicator on the back of the camera or in the LCD status display. Always be sure the focus indicator shows that the autofocus is set. A more common cause is the autofocus is locked on the wrong subject. An indication would be one part of the photo being in sharp focus. Check the scene mode settings; pictures can be blurry if you take a landscape shot with the camera set to macro mode.

Transfer Pictures to Your Computer

When the memory card is full of pictures, you can transfer them to your computer for evaluation. By learning the options for transferring and viewing your images, you can quickly and easily move images from your digital camera to your computer.

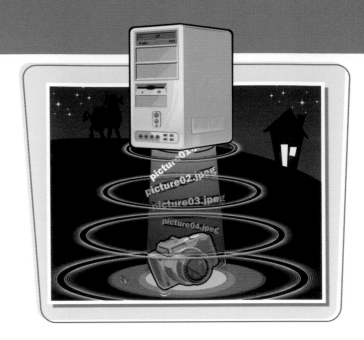

Why Transfer Pictures to Your Computer?

The LCD screen on your digital camera is small. By reviewing pictures in a larger view on your computer, you can decide whether the camera settings that you used need changing. You can use the software that came with the camera on your computer to view the pictures, or an image editing program, such as Photoshop Elements.

What About Raw-Format Images?

If you take Raw-format pictures, then you need to use the manufacturer's software or the Camera Raw plug-in feature of Photoshop Elements to view and edit your images. The Raw conversion program allows you to correct or fine-tune exposure settings including aperture and white balance. After you save the images in TIFF or JPEG format, you can open and continue editing images in programs such as Photoshop Elements or Microsoft Digital Image Pro.

Transfer Options

How you download images depends on your camera. Your camera may have a dock that plugs into your computer. You can also use a USB cable, a separately purchased memory-card reader, or a PC adapter card. Most digital cameras are recognized by computer operating systems, and they take you through the transfer process using a step-by-step wizard-style interface.

The Easiest Transfer Technique

If your camera has a docking station, the easiest way to transfer images is to plug the camera into the cradle of the docking station. The computer to which the station is attached detects the camera and begins the download. If your camera does not have a docking station, the fastest way to transfer images is to use an inexpensive memory card reader.

Disconnect Your Camera and Clear the Card

To disconnect your camera or card reader from your computer, first ensure that the access indicator light is off, and then click the **Safely Remove Hardware** icon (🔌) in the Windows taskbar. Then unplug the USB cable.

To clear the card, turn the camera on. You can delete the pictures from the memory card by choosing the **Format Card** option on one of the camera menus. Ensure that the images have been transferred safely to your computer before reformatting the memory card.

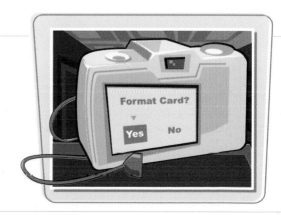

You cannot tell how good your test pictures are until you see them on a computer. This is your chance to identify any camera settings you may want to change.

Identify Recurring Issues

Evaluating your first images allows you to determine any recurring problems that require a change in your camera settings. Most problems are related to using incorrect settings for a particular shooting situation. In a few rare cases, the problems you see may represent a consistent pattern of behavior that requires correction in the camera settings to overcome.

Evaluate Exposure

Different cameras can exhibit different exposure characteristics. If all the pictures look consistently too dark, then the camera may underexpose the images, provided that you use the correct settings when you take the picture. If the pictures consistently look too light, then the camera may overexpose images, or the flash intensity is too strong.

Evaluate Color

Most cameras evaluate and adjust for white balance correctly. Providing that the camera white balance is set correctly, look for unnatural color casts in photos taken on a bright sunny day. Do not consider photos that were taken under artificial lighting as it can produce unpredictable results, including a tendency toward a warm, red cast, or a yellow or green cast. If you find that the photos consistently produce a color cast, you can often fine-tune the white balance settings, described later in the section "Fine-Tune Camera Settings."

Evaluate Saturation and Contrast

Go through your pictures and evaluate the saturation, which is the intensity of color, and the contrast, which is the difference between light and dark tones. Evaluate whether the colors are too intense or unnaturally vibrant. Be sure that your computer monitor is calibrated correctly and often, as described in Chapter 12.

Do Not Worry About Sharpness

When you look at digital pictures on a computer monitor, they may seem *soft*, not as crisp as film prints. Although you can set higher sharpening settings on most cameras, resist the urge. You can sharpen images as the last step in editing. You sharpen images based on the final image size and whether you want to print or use the picture on the Web.

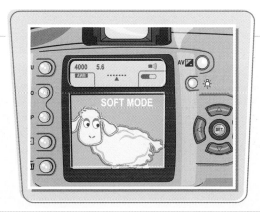

Fine-Tune Camera Settings

Most digital cameras today produce excellent exposures with good color accuracy. In some cases, fine-tuning your camera settings helps you get better photos without the need to make corrections on your computer.

Make a List of Settings to Fine-Tune

Your first foray into using the digital camera provides an overview of the camera's capabilities in normal shooting situations, using the default settings. Now you know which settings to adjust and which ones to leave as they are. Make a list of the settings you want to adjust, and then begin by making small adjustments. Then evaluate the results. Modern cameras typically produce good results and therefore you may not need to make any setting adjustments at all.

Why Fine-Tune Your Camera Settings?

You want to begin image editing with the best quality image you can get from your camera. This saves you time and makes image editing much more enjoyable. Although image editing software is powerful, it cannot fix some things, including poor focus, heavy-color casts, and overexposed images.

Fine-Tune the Flash

If flash pictures are overexposed or too light, and the cause is not a finger obstructing the flash sensor, you can adjust the flash intensity by choosing a minus setting on the camera flash menu. If you do not have a flash adjustment option, you can set a minus exposure value (EV) when you take a flash picture. You can experiment to see which setting produces the best flash photo.

Fine-Tune the Exposure

Scenes with large expanses of very dark or very light areas can fool the camera meter so that pictures are overexposed and underexposed, respectively. You can set exposure compensation, or a plus or minus exposure value (EV), to get a picture with normal tonal values.

Fine-Tune Color, Saturation, and Contrast

Newer digital cameras offer options to increase color, saturation, and contrast. Never adjust settings based on LCD images, which are too small to accurately show these characteristics. Instead, evaluate a large sampling of representative pictures on a computer and as prints. If the color, saturation, or contrast is consistently off, then adjust in small increments until you get the pictures you want.

Avoiding Digital Photography Pitfalls

In this chapter, you learn how to recognize and avoid the most common problems in digital photography.

With all the automatic features in today's digital cameras, it is still possible to take digital pictures that have problems that no amount of computer image editing can fix. You can learn the most common digital photography problems and how to avoid them.

What Are Unfixable Photo Problems?

Unfixable digital photo problems include excessively overexposed pictures, pictures with excessive *digital noise* — unwanted multicolored pixels throughout the image — and blurry pictures. Use the tips in this chapter to avoid taking unfixable pictures as well as to learn about other common digital photography problems.

You can tell if an image is properly exposed by looking at the distribution of light, medium, and dark tones shown on the image histogram on the camera or in an image editing program.

Not all digital cameras offer a histogram feature. Refer to your manual for details.

What a Histogram Shows

A histogram shows the distribution of tones, or the *contrast*, in an image. Brightness, from black (on the left) to white, appears on the horizontal axis. The vertical axis shows the number, or weight, of pixels at each brightness level. In an average scene, a well-exposed image shows tonal distribution and weight distributed fairly evenly across the entire histogram.

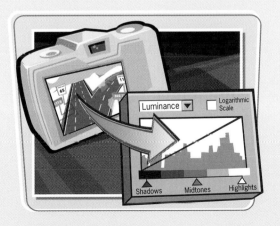

How to Identify Problem Pictures

When examining a photo's histogram on the LCD of your camera, you are looking to see if the pixels drop off sharply at either end of the histogram. A steep drop off is called *clipping* and it indicates that some of the pixels in the image are either overexposed (right side) or underexposed (left side). When pixels are clipped, they are either pushed to pure white or black and lose all detail.

Use a Histogram as You Take Pictures

Under the best conditions it is difficult to evaluate a photo on the camera's LCD screen. On digital cameras that display a histogram, you can judge whether a picture is properly exposed by looking at the histogram immediately after you take the picture.

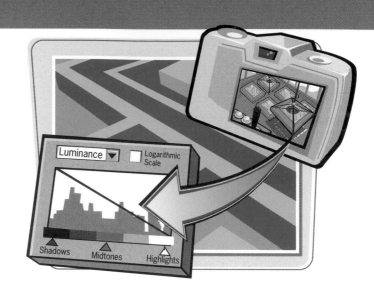

Turn On the Histogram Display

To see if your camera offers a histogram display, check the playback display options, or check the camera manual. Sometimes you may need to scroll through image information pages to get to the histogram in playback mode.

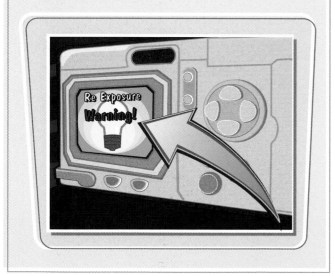

Use Overexposure Warning

Some cameras offer an LCD display mode that flashes the parts of the image that are overexposed. Some areas of an image, such as a bright, overcast sky or a white fence, can be overexposed without affecting the quality of the photo. If your camera offers a histogram display, areas of the photo that are too light appear bunched up on the right side of the display.

Does the Overexposure Warning Flash?

If the overexposure display flashes in certain areas, note the exposure settings shown. You can then move the subject to a less bright area, or choose an exposure compensation setting, such as −1.0 EV, that lets half as much light into the camera. Take the picture again and check the histogram.

Non-Average Scene Histograms

When scenes are predominately dark or light, the histogram reflects the predominate tones. For example, if you take a picture of a white wall, the pixels fall on the right side of the histogram.

High-Key Histograms

In *high-key* scenes, with mostly light tones, most of the brightness pixels fall to the right of the histogram, even with an accurate exposure, as shown here. High-key photos are popular in advertising these days but you need to ensure that areas in which the details are to be preserved are not so bright that the camera records no detail in the picture.

Low-Key Histograms

In *low-key* scenes, with mostly dark tones, most of the brightness pixels fall to the left of the histogram, even with an accurate exposure, as shown here. In low-key scenes, try to ensure that darker shadow areas retain detail by ensuring that the scene is not overexposed. You can also regain some shadow detail using the midtone adjustment in the Levels dialog box.

Compensate for Shutter Lag

Unlike film cameras that instantly take a picture when you press the shutter release button, many digital cameras delay before taking the picture. With each new model of digital camera, the amount of delay (shutter lag) gets smaller. The fact is almost all digital cameras that are not digital single lens reflex (SLR) have some degree of shutter lag. Regardless of how much shutter lag your camera has, you can learn how to work around the delay to avoid missing the action.

What Is Shutter Lag?

The delay between the time you press the shutter release button and the time when the camera takes the picture is called *shutter lag*. Because of this delay, you can miss capturing the action, such as the moment a family member blows out candles on a birthday cake, or when a basketball player moves a ball down the court.

Avoid Missing Critical Moments

To work around shutter lag, you can anticipate the action. Focus on where the action will happen and press the shutter release button halfway down, wait for the action, and then take the picture. You should also turn off red eye reduction if you use a flash, and you should remove accessory lenses and avoid using extreme zoom settings. Also switch to burst mode to capture a rapid sequence of pictures with no shutter lag.

You can fix many problems in image editing programs, but you cannot fix areas of the image where the camera records no details. You can learn how to avoid blowing out the highlight details.

What Are Blowouts?

When you take pictures in a scene with very bright and very dark areas, the brightness differences may exceed the camera's *dynamic range*, or its ability to record both very bright and very dark areas. As a result, very bright areas often lack detail and appear as solid white.

How to Avoid Blowouts

It is particularly important to avoid blowouts in the main subject area. One of the most problematic subjects is a wedding dress on a bright, sunny day. To avoid blown highlights, switch to a semi-automatic or manual mode, and then select spot or center-weighted metering. The camera meter weighs exposure primarily for light falling on the subject rather than averaging the entire scene, ensuring accurate subject exposure, as shown here. If the dress is not properly metered, it will blow out and the details of the dress will be lost.

Keep Your Camera Steady

Small, lightweight cameras invite a lot of everyday, impromptu snapshots. But the camera's light weight can also mean blurry pictures. You can learn how to get sharp pictures with small cameras.

What Is Camera Shake?

Newer pocket- and palm-size digital cameras make everyday snaps inviting and easy. Because of their low weight, avoiding *camera shake* — blur from hand movement during shooting — can be challenging. Whenever you have the zoom lens extended to telephoto, it is more susceptible to shake.

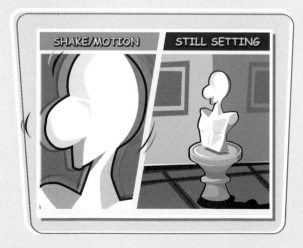

How to Avoid Camera Shake

In all but very bright scenes, you need to steady the camera by leaning against a solid surface such as a wall, or by setting the camera on a solid surface when taking the picture. Alternatively, you can buy a tabletop tripod that ensures sharp images. A simple solution is to carry a small sandwich bag filled with dried beans. It is lightweight and form-fits the camera to a fence post or a pillar.

With digital cameras, you can easily avoid taking pictures that have an unwanted color cast. Setting the camera to get accurate color also saves time when you edit images on the computer.

What Causes Undesirable Color Casts?

Modern digital cameras produce accurate color in photos automatically without using additional settings. Color casts occur when you take pictures in one type of light, such as shade, but the camera either cannot determine the color temperature of the light source or the camera is set to a type of light, such as bright sun. In the photos shown here, one was shot in automatic mode and the colors of the incandescent lights cast a warm, reddish orange. The second photo was taken with the white balance, or WB, setting deliberately set wrong to show what a difference it makes. To produce accurate colors, the camera must be set for the light in the scene. See Chapter 3 for more information about light.

Set White Balance to Get Accurate Color

When shooting outdoors, you can usually use the automatic settings with confidence. However, you may want to experiment with different white balance, or WB, settings, to become familiar with the effect that each setting produces and to help you avoid taking pictures with unnatural color casts. To set the white balance, use the camera's menu — usually the shooting menu — to select a setting that matches the scene light, such as daylight, fluorescent, or tungsten (common household light). Be careful when you use manual settings: It is easy to forget that by selecting a white balance setting, you have turned off the automatic white balance.

Never Use Digital Zoom

Although all digital cameras advertise a digital zoom capability, digital zoom produces a lower-quality picture than optical zoom.

How Digital Zoom Works

With digital zoom, the camera takes the center of the image, crops the edges, and then expands the center section to full-image size. Some cameras *interpolate*, or add pixels into the image, to bring the image to full resolution size. Because interpolation guesses where to add pixels to the image, the results are never as good as using optical zoom.

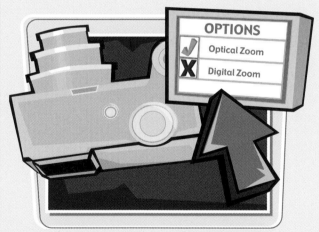

How to Avoid Using Digital Zoom

On all digital cameras that have an optical zoom, you can turn off digital zoom by selecting an option on one of the camera's menus. Most cameras with digital zoom include an audible signal or LCD indicator, to tell you when to move from optical to digital zoom. Use the indicators to avoid activating the digital zoom feature.

Digital noise is multicolor flecks or pixels in dark areas of a low-light picture or areas of solid color, such as a bright blue sky. The noise can make your digital images look grainy. You can reduce the chances of getting digital noise by following a few simple guidelines.

Recognize Digital Noise

When you take digital pictures in low-light scenes, you often see brighter, colored pixels scattered throughout the dark and shadow areas of the image. Although you may not see noise on the LCD without zooming in, you see it on the computer at 100 percent or 200 percent magnification, and in prints larger than 4 by 6 inches.

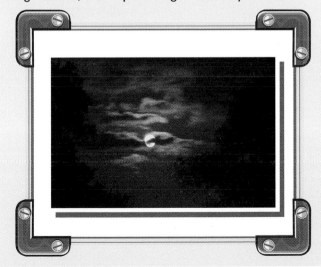

How to Avoid Digital Noise

Both high ISO settings and long exposures contribute to digital noise. Increasing the ISO setting decreases exposure times, so it is best to find a balance between the two. To reduce digital noise in low-light shots, select a higher ISO setting, such as ISO 800, and use a tripod. Take some test shots and in the LCD display zoom in as close as possible to see if the noise is excessive. Adjust the ISO settings so the shutter time remains less than 2 seconds if possible. Some cameras offer noise reduction for shutter speeds less than 1/20 of a second; this feature does not completely eliminate the noise but it does reduce it.

Avoid In-Camera Adjustments

Digital cameras offer options that let you increase or decrease picture contrast and saturation in your camera. Learn to use these adjustments cautiously, and only after evaluating test pictures to avoid an unnatural look.

Avoid High-Contrast Settings

More and more cameras offer options for adjusting image sharpness, contrast, and color saturation. Although these can be useful for snapshots, they also produce images that look artificially enhanced. If your camera offers a contrast level adjustment, you should not select the high-contrast option to avoid taking contrasted images.

Avoid Increased Saturation Settings

Options for increasing *saturation*, or intensity of colors, add vibrancy to the colors but they also produce images that look unnaturally vivid. If you want more vivid images, wait to increase saturation in an image editing program.

Camera characteristics vary by type and manufacturer. Learning your camera's characteristics and adjusting for them can produce consistently better pictures.

Fine-Tune Exposure Settings

After several weeks of taking pictures with your camera, you can tell if the camera consistently overexposes or underexposes images. You can select positive or negative exposure value (EV) settings to compensate for consistent exposure problems. For example, if your camera overexposes images (they are too light), choose a negative EV setting.

Fine-Tune White Balance and Flash Settings

Like exposure settings, you can adjust settings, such as white balance and flash intensity, on many digital cameras. For example, if you take pictures indoors under the same kind of household light, you can select a positive or negative tungsten white balance setting to get more accurate color. You can also adjust the flash to reduce the output for better flash picture results, as shown here.

Capturing Unique Photo Opportunities

There are some photographic situations that are not ordinary and require extra effort to get a satisfactory result. Whether you are taking photographs of items to sell on eBay or for insurance purposes, capturing the grandeur of a fireworks display in the evening, or shooting and creating a panorama, you can use your digital camera to get the most out of each event.

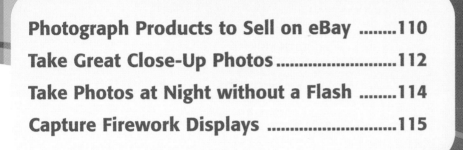

Photograph Products to Sell on eBay

Millions of people sell products on eBay every day. Many times the seller is selling a product such as a book or software of which a product shot is available online, and so the seller uses the existing photo rather than taking a photo. While this is a timesaver, products that sell best are those that include photos of the actual products. In this section, you learn the basics about how to photograph your priceless objects to get the best price for them.

Keep It Simple

Do not take a photo of an object that has a cluttered background or a background that is the same color as the subject you are photographing. You want the eyes of the potential buyer to focus on the object that you want to sell and not to be lost in the background.

Fill the Screen

Fill the screen with the subject you want to sell. If the object you are photographing is small and in the background, and the potential buyer has a difficult time examining it, he will move on to similar objects for sale.

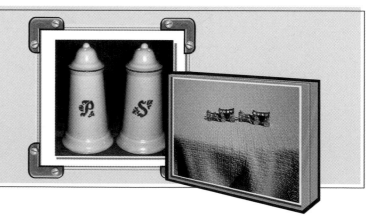

Use Props to Hold Objects Up

If the object is a book or something that typically lies flat, prop it up by putting it in a stand or by putting something behind it. Do not take a photo of it lying down because it will appear wider at the bottom and the top will be out of focus or dark.

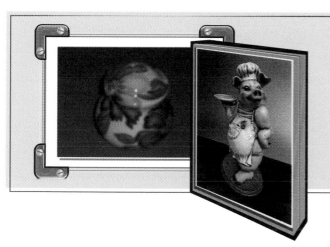

Focus, Focus, Focus

The autofocus (AF) system of a digital camera typically has a difficult time focusing under low light or when the subject is really close. Make sure your photos are in focus by viewing them on your computer and not just the LCD screen on the back of your camera. If they are out of focus, add more lighting and shoot the photos again.

Use Your Other Digital Camera

Rather than attempting to photograph objects that are small (such as stamps, coins, and so on) with a digital camera, consider putting these items on the copy glass of a scanner. Good scanners cost less than $50 and produce excellent high-resolution images.

Take Great Close-Up Photos

Close-up photography (called macro photography) opens up a whole new world of detail. With most digital cameras, it does not require any special equipment because the cameras have a macro mode built into the camera. This section covers some very simple and basic rules for taking macro photographs.

Switch the Camera to Macro Mode

Most digital cameras have a macro mode that is enabled by selecting the mode with a dial or from a menu on the LCD screen. When the camera is in macro mode, it can focus on subjects that are as close as 1 inch from the camera lens.

Get Close to Your Subject

Often the subjects of macro photography are at or near ground level. The best way to create a great photo is to get down on the ground with the subject. This allows you to steady the camera with your elbows on something solid, such as the ground.

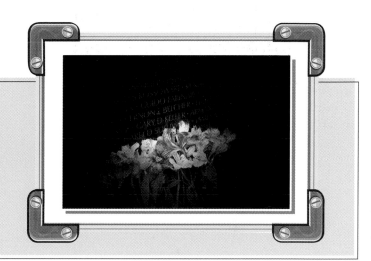

Use a Focus Light

When photographing natural subjects under low lighting conditions, the autofocus, or AF, system of the camera often has a difficult time finding the sharpest focus. If your camera does not have a built-in autofocus assist light, buy a tiny key ring flashlight at a camera or sporting goods store. They are very small and cost less than $10. This allows you to illuminate the subject with one hand while holding the camera as it is focusing with the other hand.

Depth of Field

When a camera is in macro mode, depth of field (DOF) is greatly reduced. This means that something only a few inches behind the subject may be completely out of focus. Reducing the aperture (increasing the f-stop number) can help increase the amount of area that will be in focus but it will rarely be more than a few inches in macro mode. In most cases, it produces a soft background that enhances the photo.

Take Photos at Night without a Flash

Taking photos at night without the use of flash can produce dramatic pictures; the camera changes the way areas of light and dark appear. The necessity to leave the shutter open for long periods of time to get a proper exposure produces streaks of lights as moving cars go past the camera lens. The light produced by high-pressure street lamps changes the colors of ordinary scenes into something surreal.

Use Night Mode

If your camera has a night mode setting, you should use it. Usually selected through a dial setting, the night mode usually increases the ISO (sensitivity) settings of the camera to a high level. This higher setting allows you to take photos without a flash but it also increases the amount of noise in the photo.

Keep Your Camera Steady

If your subject is stationary, you can take a photo under low lighting conditions by stabilizing your camera. In most cases, this means using a tripod, but a camera placed on a bean bag on something solid will work just as well. The only problem with this approach is if the subject moves — your steady camera is of no use then.

Firework displays dazzle viewers but can be a real challenge for the digital photographer to capture. Although the lights in the sky are beautiful to the human eye, they are dim to the digital camera and confuse many of the mechanisms in the camera such as autofocus and light metering. A few digital cameras actually have a fireworks shooting mode, but most do not. Here are some basic things to know about photographing fireworks.

Capture Firework Displays

SET UP YOUR CAMERA

1 Set up your camera on a tripod.

2 Turn off your camera's flash.

3 Set the focus mode to landscape.

Note: This turns off the automatic focus, or AF, and sets the focus to infinity.

4 Set the shutter speed to bulb.

Note: If your camera does not have a bulb setting, use a one-second setting.

CAPTURE A BURST OF FIREWORKS

5 Aim the camera at the area you expect the fireworks to explode.

6 Wait until you hear the sound of a firework being launched (a dull thump).

7 If you use a bulb setting, push your shutter button down and hold it.

Note: If your camera has a remote shutter control, you can use it to prevent any jiggling caused by the pressure from your finger on the shutter button.

8 When the burst has completely finished, release the shutter.

Note: For cameras without a bulb setting, press the shutter button after the explosion has started.

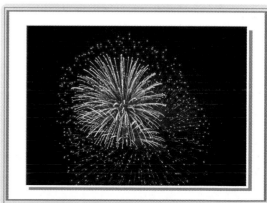

Organizing Photos in Photoshop Elements

One of the many benefits of owning and using a digital camera is the ability to take an almost unlimited number of photos without incurring additional costs, such as film and processing fees. You can take and download so many photos to your computer that sorting and organizing them is often challenging. In this chapter, you discover how to use the Organizer workspace in Photoshop Elements to sort and organize your photos so that it is easy to view and find a particular photo.

Why Use Image Editing Programs?

Image editing programs allow you to view and modify photographic images. You are able to open your digital photos, as well as crop, color correct, and enhance them. With some image editing applications, you can even create special effects, add text, and convert images to different formats for various uses.

Image Editing Programs

You can choose from a variety of image editing programs. In fact, many digital cameras and photo printers include a simple image editing program. Such bundled programs are usually more limited in scope than those that are purchased separately. Instead of trying multiple image editors, such as the ones that came with the camera and printer, using a more comprehensive application makes downloading, fixing, and sharing your photos much easier.

Use a Complete Image Editing Program

Although it is often bundled with hardware such as a Wacom digitizing tablet and some scanners, Photoshop Elements is considered a stand-alone image editing program. It is the most popular program available and because it is based on the most widely used professional image editor — Photoshop — it is also a powerful and versatile program. Photoshop Elements not only allows you to download images to your computer, correct photo problems, and apply special effects, it also includes a photo organizer that simplifies the task of viewing and organizing your digital images.

Enhance Digital Photos with Photoshop Elements

Using Photoshop Elements, you can fix red eye and correct the color, contrast, and saturation in your digital photos. You can also remove or add elements, such as people or objects. Elements can help you prepare and print your photos on your home photo printer, or send them for printing to a commercial photo lab. Elements can also help you easily resize pictures and attach them to e-mails to send to friends and family.

Change Ordinary Photos into Digital Creations

With Photoshop Elements, you can easily add text to a picture and turn any photo into a greeting card. You can use your favorite photos to create a personalized calendar or create a slide show from any group of photos and save it with music and transitions.

Why Use an Organizing System for Digital Photos?

When you start taking photos with a digital camera, the number of photos you take will increase dramatically. It is not unusual to take more than 100 photos at a birthday party or other event. With so many photos, you need a way to sort, group, and save them in specific locations on your hard drive or external media.

Stay Organized with Photoshop Elements

You can import photos from your camera directly into the Organizer workspace in Elements and categorize or tag them for easy reference. You can then use the Photo Browser in the Organizer workspace to find and view specific photos while keeping them in their original location on your hard drive.

What Is a Digital Editing Workflow?

A digital editing workflow is a sequence of steps for importing, organizing, editing, and sharing your digital images. Following a workflow that fits your particular needs ensures that all your photos are imported, reviewed, organized, corrected, or enhanced, and prepared for sharing in a simple, straightforward manner.

Import and Organize Your Photos

The first steps of the digital workflow include moving the photos from your camera to your computer, reviewing the photos, assigning tags that can be used to identify them, and grouping them into collections — which are similar to traditional photo albums with photos grouped by themes.

The Editing Process

The next steps include making changes to the photos to correct image rotation, removing defects such as red eye, and making adjustments to color and lighting. At this stage, you can also make other enhancements such as removing objects or people from a picture, creating a composite of several pictures, and adding text or special effects.

Make Digital Photo Creations

Optionally, you can use any photo to create special greeting cards or postcards, design photo calendars, and put together slide shows and photo albums.

Output Photos for Print, CD, DVD, the Web, and E-mail

The final step of the digital workflow is to print your images or creations or share them by burning a CD or DVD, making a Web photo gallery, or sending photos as e-mail attachments.

The Welcome Screen Choices in Photoshop Elements

When you launch Photoshop Elements, the first thing you see is a welcome screen. From this starting point, you select what you plan to do and Elements starts the application with the corresponding workspace. Hovering the cursor over each icon choice opens a subscreen with a simple description.

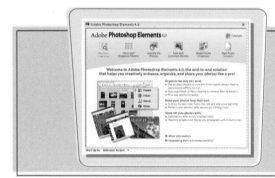

Product Overview

The product overview is a quick way to familiarize yourself with everything you can do with Photoshop Elements. This icon is simply informational. From this screen, you can get information on the application in general or click **Upgrading from a previous version** and learn what has changed since the previous version.

View and Organize Photos

When you click **View and Organize Photos**, Photoshop Elements starts with the Organizer workspace and the Photo Browser. From here you can import, view, and sort your photos.

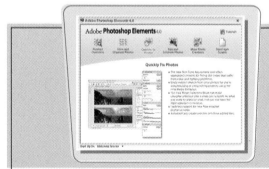

Quickly Fix Photos

When you click **Quickly Fix Photos**, the application launches into the Quick Fix mode of the Editor workspace. You can open individual photos and make quick corrections, while comparing your changes with the original image.

Edit and Enhance Photos

Clicking **Edit and Enhance Photos** opens Photoshop Elements in the main Editor workspace called Standard Edit. In this mode, you can open, improve, and add text and special effects to your photos, using all the possibilities of this powerful image editor.

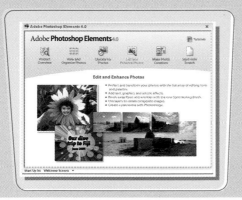

Make Photo Creations

When you click **Make Photo Creations**, Elements launches into the Organizer with a Creation Setup screen superimposed. You select the type of creation you want to make, such as a slide show or a calendar page. When you click **OK**, you follow the on-screen steps to select the styles and photos for your creation.

Start from Scratch

Click **Start From Scratch** to launch Photoshop Elements in Standard Edit mode with the New dialog box automatically opened so you can select the name, size, and color for your new page.

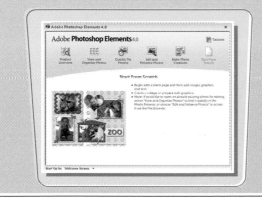

Tutorials

Clicking **Tutorials** launches your Web browser and links you directly to the Adobe Tips Web site where you can view a number of useful tips and tutorials for using Photoshop Elements.

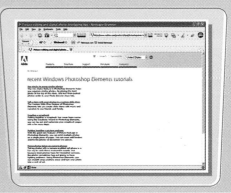

Understanding the Organizer Workspace

The Organizer in Photoshop Elements is used at the beginning and end of your digital workflow. It can help you organize photos and other media files including music files, and has the tools to import, review, sort, and create cool projects using your photos.

Shortcuts Bar
In addition to a normal menu bar, the Organizer includes a shortcuts bar for quickly moving between different tasks in Photoshop Elements.

Photo Browser
Displays your photos as thumbnails at any size you select.

Status Bar
Shows the number of items selected.

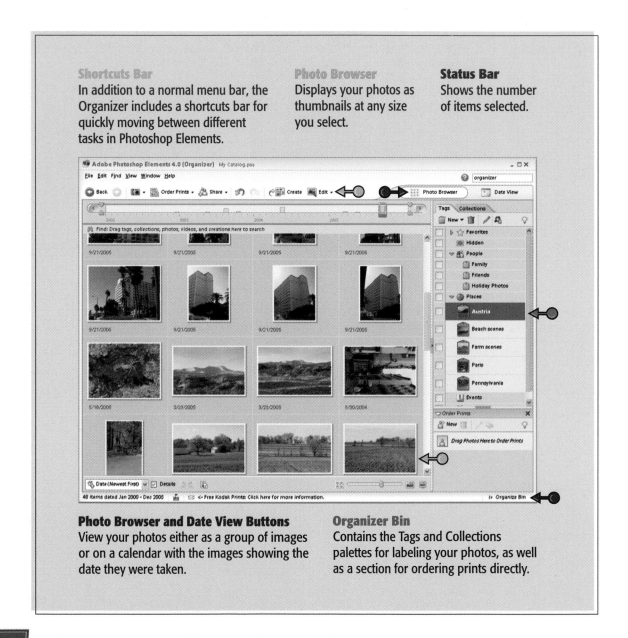

Photo Browser and Date View Buttons
View your photos either as a group of images or on a calendar with the images showing the date they were taken.

Organizer Bin
Contains the Tags and Collections palettes for labeling your photos, as well as a section for ordering prints directly.

Move Photos into Your Computer (Step 1)

When you plug your camera or card reader into your computer, the Photo Downloader automatically launches and searches for new images. You can select a folder to store the photos and optionally change the filenames. When you click **Get Photos**, the downloader automatically downloads them into the Organizer. You can also launch Photoshop Elements and select **Get Photos** from the menu to start the process manually.

Review the Photos (Step 2)

After copying the photos into your computer, you can sort through your photos and delete any that are out of focus, underexposed, overexposed, or that you just do not want. The Photo Organizer provides a full-screen preview to review your photos and includes the ability to view different photos side by side for comparisons.

Add Tags to Photos (Step 3)

After you have removed the undesirable photos and identified the ones you want to keep, the next step is to attach tags to those photos to identify them. Photos can have multiple tags. For example, a photo of Bob on vacation in Hawaii may have the following tags attached: Family, Bob, Hawaii, or Vacation. Tagging your photos is an important part of maintaining an organized image library.

Group Images into Collections (Step 4)

You can further organize your photos into collections, which are similar to digital photo albums. You can group photos with different tags into the same collection and even save the photos in any order within the collection.

Understanding Metadata in Your Photos

One of the unique features of photos taken with digital cameras is that there is a lot of information about the camera settings and more stored with each image. When you release the shutter on a digital camera, it records more than just the scene you captured. The camera attaches descriptive data known as *metadata* to each image file on the digital media card. Many different types of data can be attached to an image. Some cameras even provide a Global Positioning System (GPS) receiver connection, thereby precisely pinpointing the location where the photograph was taken.

What Is EXIF?

EXIF stands for Exchangeable Image File Format. It is the most commonly used metadata. It was developed to standardize the exchange of data between imaging devices such as a camera and software. EXIF is the information that is stored by the camera with each photo and includes the date and time, the make and model of the camera, the white balance settings, whether the flash was used, and other details about the image capture.

Personalize Metadata

You can add your own information to the file's metadata to help identify and organize your images. When you add titles, tags, and descriptions in the Organizer, Photoshop Elements stores that data with the photo file. In fact, when you edit photos in Elements, the edit history is also added to the metadata.

Most high-end digital cameras can save photos in a format called *Raw*. The term Raw is not an acronym. It means that the image data coming off the camera sensor is not processed or compressed before being saved to the memory card. Although Raw format files are larger than JPEG files, they give the photographer more control over exposure, color, and tonal correction of the photo when it is processed on the computer.

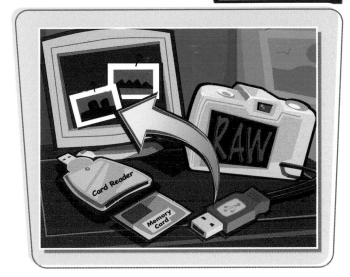

Processing Raw Format Digital Photos

Before you can use a Raw format file on your computer, you must first convert it into a standard graphics format. There are several ways to process Raw digital photos on your computer. You can use conversion software provided by the camera manufacturer, use a third-party conversion program, or you can use the Raw file conversion software that is now included in many popular image editors. Regardless of the process you choose, the end result is an image in a format that can be used with your image editor.

Advantages of Raw Format

When you take a photo using a JPEG format, the image sensor data is processed using the camera's current white balance, exposure, contrast, saturation, and many other settings. After the JPEG image is saved to the memory card, these settings cannot be changed. When an image is saved as a Raw file, the actual data produced by the photo sensor is stored on the memory card. The photographer can then visually control the color and tonal corrections as he or she processes the image on the computer. The advantages of such controlled processing easily outweigh the extra steps required to process a Raw image and its larger file size, which reduces the number of images that can be stored on one memory card.

Create a New Catalog and Import Photos

When you bring photos or any other media files into Photoshop Elements, a catalog called My Catalog is automatically created. You can use that one catalog to store all your files, or you can create multiple catalogs with specific names.

Create a New Catalog and Import Photos

CREATE A NEW CATALOG

① Launch Photoshop Elements in the Organizer workspace.

② Click **File**.

③ Click **Catalog**.

The Catalog dialog box appears.

④ Click **New**.

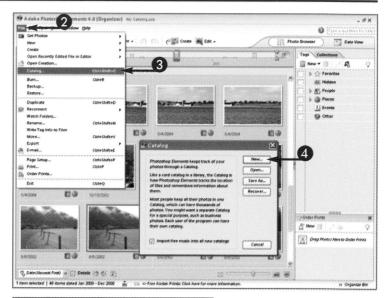

The New Catalog dialog box appears.

⑤ Click the **Save in** ⊡ and select a location for the catalog.

⑥ Type a name for the catalog in the **File name** text box.

*Note: Do not type **My Catalog** or you will overwrite the default catalog and any images already stored there.*

⑦ Click **Save**.

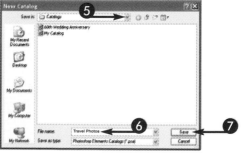

Photoshop Elements creates and opens a new empty catalog.

IMPORT PHOTOS

8 Click in the shortcuts bar.

9 Select **From Camera or Card Reader**.

● If the photos are already on your hard drive, select **From Files and Folders** and use the dialog box that appears to navigate to the folder on your hard drive to select the images to import.

The Adobe Photoshop Elements – Photo Downloader dialog box appears.

10 Click the **Get Photos from** ▼ and select the card reader.

11 Click **Get Photos**.

Photoshop Elements copies all the photos to the open catalog.

Photoshop Elements then asks if you want to delete those files from your camera or card reader.

12 Click **No**.

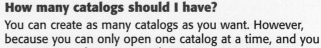

Note: It is always best to format the memory card in the digital camera after you have downloaded the files to the computer. Formatting erases all the images on the card and prepares the card to record photos from that particular camera. If you delete files using the computer, you can encounter memory card problems because bits of data may be left on the card.

TIPS

What is a catalog?
A catalog is a list of thumbnails and the data stored with them. It does not contain the actual photos themselves. You can also import music files into a catalog. You can browse through one catalog and see all the images wherever they are located on the hard drive, even if they are stored in separate folders or located on separate hard drives.

How many catalogs should I have?
You can create as many catalogs as you want. However, because you can only open one catalog at a time, and you cannot move photos or tags between catalogs, Adobe recommends keeping all your photos in a single catalog. You can keep separate images grouped using the Tags and Collections palettes. See the tasks "Organize with Tags" and "Organize with Collections," both later in this chapter, for more.

Review, Compare, and Sort Your Photos

After the photos are in your computer and have been added to the catalog, the next step is to carefully review them, compare similar images, and decide which ones should be kept and which should not. Why not keep all of them? Photos take up space on your hard drive, so keeping photos that you do not need wastes your time — when looking through the catalog — and occupies space on your hard drive.

Review, Compare, and Sort Your Photos

① Launch Photoshop Elements in the Organizer workspace.

② Click a photo thumbnail.

③ Click **View**.

④ Click **View Photos in Full Screen**.

The photo fills the screen, and the Full Screen View Options dialog box appears.

⑤ Select **Show Filmstrip** (☐ changes to ✓).

⑥ Click **OK**.

The photo fills the screen with a filmstrip on the right showing all the photo thumbnails.

7 Click another photo in the filmstrip.

8 Repeat Step **7** to review other photos.

9 Move the cursor to the top of the screen.

A control bar appears.

10 Click the **Side by Side View** button (▦).

TIPS

How can I rotate a photo?
Click the **Rotate 90° Left** icon (▣) or the **Rotate 90° Right** icon (▣) in the control bar for the comparison view. If you are in the Organizer's Photo Browser, the same Rotate icons are on the bottom of the Browser window.

How do I return to the Photo Browser window?
Click the **Exit-Esc** icon (▣) to return to the main Photo Browser window in the Organizer. You can also press Esc on your keyboard to exit the Comparison or Full Screen view and return to the Photo Browser.

continued

Being able to compare two similar photos side by side is particularly useful when taking photos of people. You can instantly decide which one best captures the personality or the moment, or quickly delete any images where the subject's eyes are closed or the smile is crooked.

Review, Compare, and Sort Your Photos *(continued)*

Two images appear on-screen.

⑪ Click the left image to select it.

⑫ Click a photo in the filmstrip to view as a comparison.

⑬ Click the right image to select it.

⑭ Click a second photo in the filmstrip to view as a comparison.

The two images are viewed side by side.

⑮ Click a photo you want to delete.

⑯ Move the cursor to the top of the screen to view the toolbar.

⑰ Click the **Delete** icon (🗑).

The Confirm Deletion from Catalog dialog box appears, telling you that the photo you selected will be deleted from the catalog.

● You can select this option to delete the photo from the hard drive as well (☐ changes to ☑).

⑱ Click **OK**.

The next photo in the filmstrip appears.

⑲ Repeat Steps **13** to **18** until only the photos you want to keep are left in the filmstrip.

TIPS

Can I zoom in to a photo in Comparison view?

Yes. Click a photo to select it. Then click the **Zoom in** (🔍) or **Zoom out** (🔍) icon in the control bar or click and drag the slider between them to zoom in or out. Click and drag directly in the enlarged photo. ⬉ changes to ✋ as you move around the image.

Can I zoom in and move around both photos at once?

Yes. Click the **Sync Pan and Zoom** icon (🔗) to link the two images. Then click and drag the zoom slider to zoom in and out of both photos at once. Click and drag in one photo (⬉ changes to ✋) to move around both images at once.

After the photos are reviewed and sorted, you can assign *tags*, keywords you assign to photos, and group them by subject without manually moving them into separate folders. Tags are grouped under categories, such as People or Places, and make it easy for you to locate a single photo or a group of related photos in a large image catalog.

Organize with Tags

① Launch Photoshop Elements in the Organizer workspace.

② Click the **Tags** palette in the Organizer Bin.

③ Click the **New** ▾ and select **New Tag**.

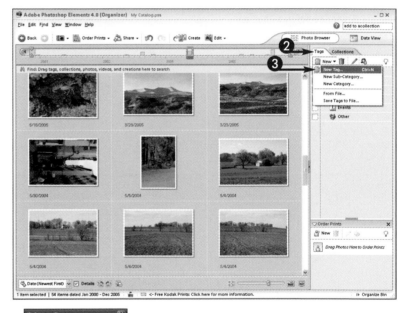

The Create Tag dialog box appears.

④ Click the **Category** ☑ and select a category.

⑤ Click in the **Name** data field, and type a tag name.

⑥ Click **OK**.

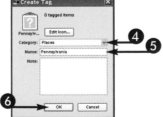

● The new tag is listed in the **Tags** palette.

ASSIGN THE TAG TO PHOTOS

⑦ Click and drag the tag over the first photo you want to assign.

Note: The first photo selected for each tag appears in the Tag icon.

⑧ Repeat Step **7** for each photo to group with the new tag.

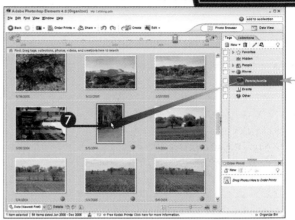

FIND PHOTOS BY TAGS

⑨ Click the box next to the tag.

The box fills with a binoculars icon (🔍).

Only the photos with that tag assigned appear in the Photo Browser window.

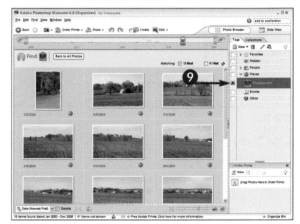

Can a photo have multiple tags?

Yes. You can create tags for any type of content, so a photo can have multiple tags. You can easily remove one or more tags from a photo by right-clicking the Tag icon under the photo and selecting **Remove the category tag** from the menu that appears.

What is face tagging?

Elements can help you by isolating all the faces in the photos in a catalog so you can tag them more quickly. Click the **Find Faces** icon (😊) in the **Tags** palette. Photoshop Elements finds and displays thumbnails of all the faces so you can quickly create and assign tags to those images.

Organize with Collections

You can group your photos into collections. Collections allow you to view all the photos as you would in a traditional photo album. For example, you might have your Hawaii vacation photos in one collection and your European vacation photos in another collection. Photos in a collection are automatically numbered as you put them into the collection. If you change the position of the photos to view them in a different order, all the thumbnails will be renumbered accordingly.

Organize with Collections

① Launch Photoshop Elements in the Organizer workspace.

② Click the **Collections** tab in the Organizer Bin.

③ Click the **New** ▾ and select **New Collection**.

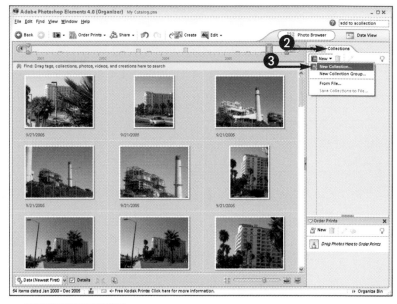

The Create Collection dialog box appears.

④ Click in the **Name** data field and type a name for the collection.

⑤ Click **OK**.

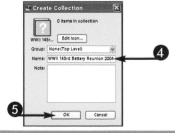

● A new collection with a question mark icon appears in the Collections palette.

ADD PHOTOS TO THE COLLECTION

6 Click and drag the new collection's icon over the first photo in the Photo Browser that belongs in this collection.

7 Repeat Step **6** for all the photos to be included in the collection.

You can also add photos to the collection by clicking and dragging one or more photos over the new collection's icon in the Collections palette.

The icon in the Collections palette shows a thumbnail of the first photo in the new collection.

VIEW PHOTOS IN THE COLLECTION

8 Click the box next to the collection.

The box fills with a binoculars icon ().

Only the photos in the new collection appear in the Photo Browser window, and each photo is numbered.

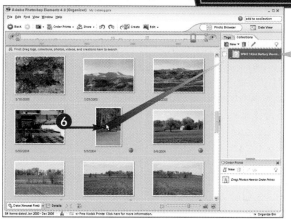

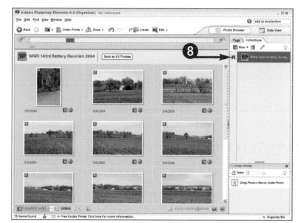

TIPS

Can I use photos with different tags in the same collection?

Yes. Collection photos can have different tags and a photo can be included in several collections. You can even attach tags to photos while you are viewing them in a collection. With the collection open in the Photo Browser, click the **Tags** palette and click and drag a tag over one or more photos in the collection.

How do I change the order of the photos in a collection?

Click the box next to the collection's name in the **Collections** palette to view all the images. Click and drag a photo in the collection to another location in the Photo Browser. Release the mouse when the cursor is where you want to view that photo in the collection.

CHAPTER 12

Fixing Photos

You can make all your photos look better with Photoshop Elements. Start by adjusting your monitor to better display your photos. Then you can crop, improve the color and contrast, remove red eye, and tint or change color images to black and white for a special effect. This chapter introduces the basics of digital image editing.

Why Calibrate and Profile Your Monitor?

Your monitor is used for viewing your photos. If your monitor is dull or changes the colors that are in the image, you cannot accurately edit your photos for color or tone. You can calibrate and profile your monitor for more accurate color. This section and the task that follows explain why and how to get better color from your monitor.

What Are Calibration and Profiling?

When you calibrate your monitor, you check and compare the color values it displays to a known standard. You then create a profile or a description of how your monitor displays color at that particular moment.

Why Should I Calibrate and Profile My Monitor?

You need the monitor to show consistent and predictable color so you can more accurately view and color correct your images. Making sure the monitor is as accurate as possible also helps ensure that the print reflects the colors you see on-screen.

Different Kinds of Monitors

CRTs and LCDs are the two basic types of computer monitors. A CRT uses a cathode ray tube and is more like a traditional TV. An LCD is a flat panel display, which uses liquid crystals in the viewing area. Both can be calibrated and profiled with hardware and software methods, however, CRTs generally require a warm-up time of 30 minutes before proceeding.

Calibration and Profiling Methods

You can use either a software-only method or a hardware-software combination to calibrate and profile. With the software-only methods, your eyes are the determining factor in judging the accuracy of the color as displayed on the monitor screen. Using a hardware device called a colorimeter along with its corresponding software is far more accurate. The colorimeter measures the actual output of color. The software with both methods produces the profile, a data file describing how your particular monitor shows colors as compared to a known ICC, or International Color Consortium, standard. The video card inside your computer uses the new profile to compensate for your monitor and to display the color according to the standard.

The Software "Eyeball" Method

You can use the Adobe Gamma software automatically installed with Photoshop Elements to calibrate and create a monitor profile. Because your eyes are the measuring tool with this method, you should dim the lights to avoid reflections on-screen. You should also wear neutral colors such as gray or black so that no colors reflect from the screen and change your color vision.

Hardware Methods

Using a hardware colorimeter to calibrate and profile your monitor is easier and results in more consistent color. The device is small, attaches to the monitor while you calibrate and profile, and reads color patches that its software produces on-screen. GretagMacbeth's Eye-One and X-Rite's Optix are excellent colorimeters.

Calibrate and Profile with Adobe Gamma

Using Adobe Gamma to calibrate and profile your monitor is a simple first step for making your photos look better both onscreen and in print. Make sure you are wearing neutral-colored clothing, that the lights in the room are dim, and that there are no external reflections on-screen. If you have a CRT monitor, make sure it has been running for at least 30 minutes before starting this task.

This task can only describe the general settings in the steps that follow because the calibration wizard includes specific choices that depend on your type of computer and monitor.

Calibrate and Profile with Adobe Gamma

MAKE THE BACKGROUND A NEUTRAL GRAY

① Click **Start**.

② Click **Control Panel**.

The Control Panel window opens.

Note: Depending on how you have set up your computer, you may access the Control Panel another way.

③ Double-click **Display**.

The Display Properties dialog box appears.

④ Click the **Desktop** tab.

⑤ Click **None** for the background.

⑥ Click the **Color** ⏷ and then click a neutral gray.

⑦ Click **Apply**.

⑧ Click **OK**.

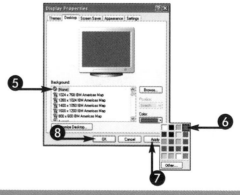

START THE ADOBE GAMMA WIZARD

9 From the Control Panel window, double-click **Adobe Gamma**.

The Adobe Gamma dialog box appears.

10 Click ⊠ to close the Control Panel window.

11 Click **Step By Step (Wizard)** (◯ changes to ◉).

12 Click **Next**.

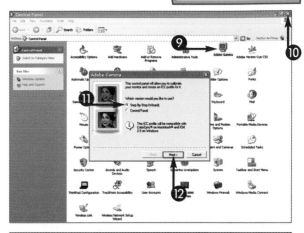

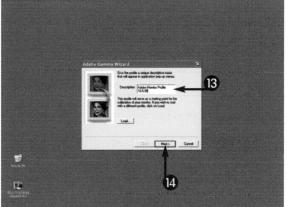

The Control Panel closes, showing the neutral gray background you chose in Step **6**.

13 Type a name and the date in the **Description** data field.

14 Click **Next**.

15 Follow the next seven on-screen steps in the Adobe Gamma Wizard to create, save, and apply the new monitor profile.

TIPS

Should I change the other monitor settings?

Yes. You should always use your monitor with the greatest number of colors it can display. Double-click the **Display** icon in the Control Panel. In the Display Properties dialog box, click the **Settings** tab. Make sure your monitor is set to **Highest (32 bit)** for color quality or at least to **Medium (16 bit)**.

Should I use the buttons on the front of my monitor?

If you have buttons or knobs on your monitor to control brightness and contrast, set these to the middle position before starting the Adobe Gamma Wizard. The wizard's on-screen steps direct you to change your brightness and contrast settings using these buttons as you proceed through the steps.

Open the Photoshop Elements Quick Fix Workspace

Photoshop Elements includes two Editor workspaces that you can open directly from the Welcome screen or from within the Organizer. The two workspaces are the Quick Fix workspace and the Standard Edit workspace. You can use either one, or start with the Quick Fix to make changes to an image, and then move on to the Standard Edit to make further enhancements. This task shows you two ways to open the Quick Fix workspace.

Open the Photoshop Elements Quick Fix Workspace

USE THE WELCOME SCREEN

1. Launch Photoshop Elements.

2. In the Welcome screen, click **Quickly Fix Photos** to open the Quick Fix workspace.

• You can click **Edit and Enhance Photos** to open the Standard Edit workspace.

Photoshop Elements opens in the Quick Fix Editor workspace.

USE THE ORGANIZER

1. Launch Photoshop Elements.

2. In the Welcome screen, click **View and Organize Photos** to open the Organizer.

Photoshop Elements opens in the Organizer.

3. Click the **Edit** ⌄ and then select **Go to Quick Fix** to open the Quick Fix Editor workspace.

• You can select **Go to Standard Edit** to open the Standard Edit workspace.

The Quick Fix Editor workspace appears.

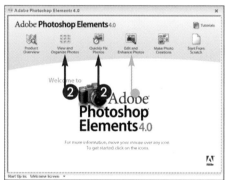

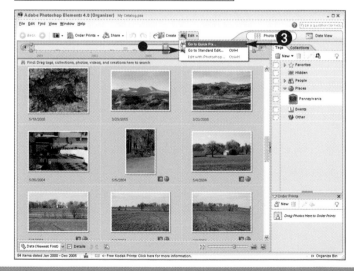

The Quick Fix workspace offers simple and easy-to-use tools for making basic photo edits and comparing the changes you make side by side with the original photo. You can view and move around the image at various sizes, correct red eye, make a variety of color and tonal enhancements, crop, and sharpen all from this workspace.

Access the Tools

Using the tools on the left side of the image window, you can zoom in and out of the photo, move around a zoomed-in image, select a specific area to change, crop the image for composition, and fix red eye quickly.

Change Your View

In the area below the main image window, you can select a before and after view, change the orientation to portrait or landscape, rotate the image, and change the zoom percentage.

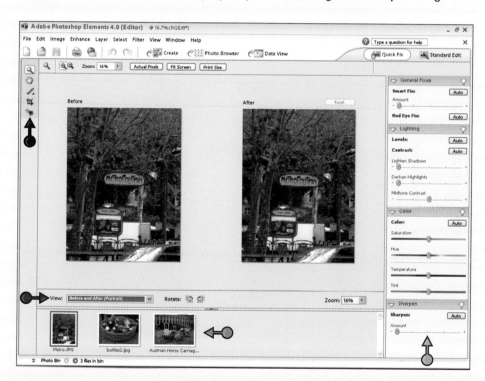

View All Open Photos

The Photo Bin shows thumbnails of all the open images. You can easily switch between images in the main window by clicking another image in the Photo Bin. Use the Previous and Next buttons (◙ and ◙) in the status bar to navigate among your open photos. You can click the Photo Bin down arrow (≡) in the status bar to hide the Photo Bin, and you can enlarge the bin by clicking and dragging the arrow (▬) on the separator bar between the bin and the main window.

Make Quick Fixes

Try the Auto fixes on the right side of the screen. Starting at the top, apply one Auto control to see if it makes the color and tonal changes you want. You can click the Reset button and try the next Auto control for a different effect. The Sharpen control is always applied last on any image.

Open a Photo to Fix

You can open almost any image on your hard drive with Photoshop Elements. You can also open several photos at once, or open a recently viewed photo without navigating to the location where the photo is stored.

Open a Photo to Fix

OPEN ONE OR MORE IMAGES

1 Click **File**.

2 Click **Open**.

*Note: You can also click the **Open** button ( ).*

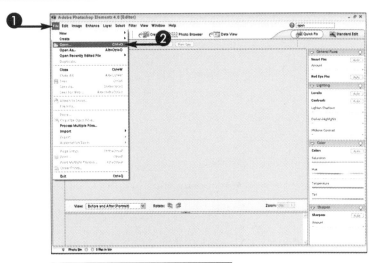

The Open dialog box appears.

3 Click the **Look in** to display additional folders.

4 Click the file you want to open.

5 Click **Open**.

*Note: Shift +click files in a series or Ctrl +click multiple separate files and click **Open** to open them all at once.*

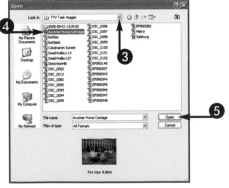

● Photoshop Elements opens the image.

● The image also appears in the Photo Bin.

OPEN A RECENTLY EDITED PHOTO

① Click **File**.

② Click **Open Recently Edited File**.

③ Click the name of the photo from the list.

● Photoshop Elements opens the image.

● The image also appears in the Photo Bin.

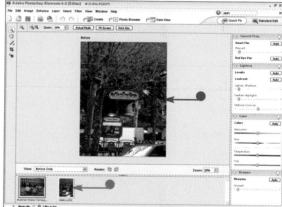

TIP

What types of files can Elements open?

Elements can open most of the common image file formats in use today. You can specify the ones you want Elements to open. From the menu, select **Edit** and then **File Association**. In the File Association Manager dialog box that appears, select any of the file types (☐ changes to ☑) you want Elements to open. Alternatively, you can click **Select All**, and Elements is now set to open all the file types listed.

File Type	Description
JPEG (Joint Photographic Experts Group)	The standard format for digital photos.
TIFF (Tagged Image Format File)	The industry standard graphics file format.
PSD (Photoshop Document)	Native file format for Photoshop and Photoshop Elements.
BMP (Bitmap)	A Windows image format.
GIF (Graphics Interchange Format)	A format for Web images with limited colors.
Raw (unprocessed camera sensor data)	Unique format that must be converted to a standard graphics format before the image can be used.

Open a Raw Photo File

Raw images are different from other images produced by a digital camera. The Camera Raw file format includes all the original digital data as it is captured by the camera's sensor. Because a Raw file has not been processed or compressed, you can use Photoshop Elements to set the white balance, tonal range, contrast, saturation, and sharpening for your requirements.

Photoshop Elements saves a sidecar file labeled .xmp with each Raw photo you open. The original file is not overwritten. When you click *Save* in the Raw dialog box, you can save the file with another name and format. When you click *Open*, you open the file to continue editing it in Photoshop Elements.

Open a Raw Photo File

① Click **File**.

② Click **Open**.

The Open dialog box appears.

③ Click the photo file.

④ Click **Open**.

The dialog box for the Raw file from your camera opens.

● You can use these tools to change the view for adjusting the image:

    🔍   Zoom tool

    ✋   Hand tool

    ✎   Color Sampler tool

    ↺   Rotate Counterclockwise

    ↻   Rotate Clockwise

⑤ In this example, click ↻ to rotate the image.

● You can use these options to adjust settings.

Note: *The Auto options, which are selected by default, are not always the best for your photo. You can move the sliders to adjust your specific image.*

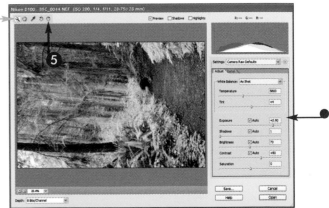

6 In this example, click the **White Balance** ▼ and select a different white balance.

7 Click **Open**.

The file opens in Elements with the Raw settings applied.

TIPS

Can I change my mind and reprocess the file after it is converted?

Yes. When you select **Open** in the Raw dialog box, Photoshop Elements saves your changes and creates a new image as it opens the Raw photo. You can reprocess the original Raw file in different ways as many times as you like and get multiple versions from the same original image capture.

Can all digital cameras produce Raw files?

No. Only some point-and-shoot digital cameras have a Raw setting. However, most prosumer cameras and all professional digital cameras or digital SLR — single lens reflex — cameras allow you to capture and save Raw files. You must set this option in the camera's shooting preferences.

When editing images, you can zoom in on certain areas to see them better and then zoom back out to view the whole image. You can change views quickly and efficiently using the Zoom tool along with certain keyboard keys and the options in the Options bar.

Zoom In and Out

① Open a photo in the Quick Fix workspace.

② Click the **Zoom** tool (

).

    ⌖ changes to ⊕.

③ Click and drag ⊕ to create a zoom marquee over a specific area.

    If you press and hold the spacebar after you start to click and drag, the zoom marquee moves to another area.

    You can also click anywhere in the image to arbitrarily zoom in.

    Press and hold the **Alt** key to temporarily change ⊕ to ⊖.

    Elements zooms in on the area you selected in Step **3**.

④ Click **Fit Screen** to make the entire image fit in the screen.

● Click **Actual Pixels** to view the image at 100 percent.

● Double-click the **Zoom** tool to automatically zoom the image to 100 percent.

● **Print Size** shows an approximate printed size depending on the actual document size and the size and resolution of your monitor.

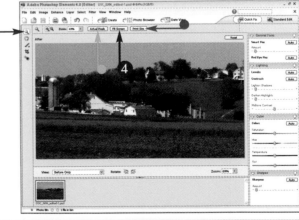

When you zoom in to work on an area, you may need to move around in the image using the zoomed-in state. You can use the Hand tool to move around easily. You can also use the keyboard keys to switch between the Hand tool and the Zoom tool to make moving around the image much quicker.

Move Around the Image

1 Open a photo in the Quick Fix workspace.

2 Click the **Hand** tool ( ).

  changes to .

3 Click and drag in the zoomed-in image.

4 Press and hold the Ctrl key to temporarily change to .

You can press and hold the Alt key to temporarily change to .

You can also press the spacebar to temporarily access the **Hand** tool ( ) when the **Zoom** tool ( ) is selected.

Rotate an Image

Your digital photo files likely include images shot both horizontally and vertically. You can easily rotate any image in Photoshop Elements using either a menu selection or a shortcut button. You can even use the Rotate menu command to flip an image either horizontally or vertically.

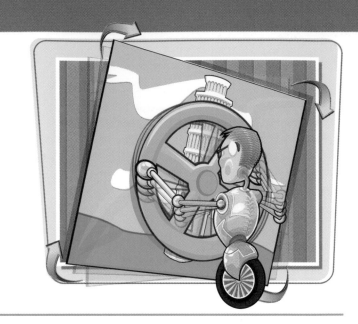

Rotate an Image

① Open a photo in the Quick Fix workspace.

② Click **Image**.

③ Click **Rotate**.

④ Click a degree of rotation.

● You can click **Flip Horizontal** or **Flip Vertical** to reverse the image.

● Elements rotates the photo.

● You can also click the left or right **Rotate Shortcut** button (and).

Select a Comparative View

Being able to compare the original photo with your edited version makes your work more efficient and effective. You can easily set the Quick Fix workspace to display two versions of the photo at once, and dynamically update the after version as you make changes.

Select a Comparative View

1 Open a photo in the Quick Fix workspace.

2 Click the **View** ⬇ and select **Before and After (Portrait)**.

● You can select **Before and After (Landscape)** depending on the photo.

● Photoshop Elements displays two identical images side by side for Portrait.

The photos appear above and below for Landscape.

Note: *When you close Photoshop Elements, the view that is in use becomes the default view when you open Elements again.*

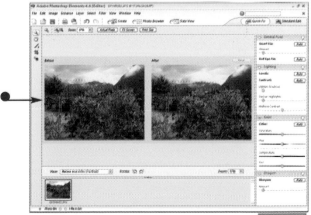

Improve Composition by Cropping

You can remove parts of an image, such as parts of a distracting background, to help focus your image and improve your composition. Using the Crop tool in Photoshop Elements, you can crop to arbitrary dimensions or you can specify the width, height, and resolution.

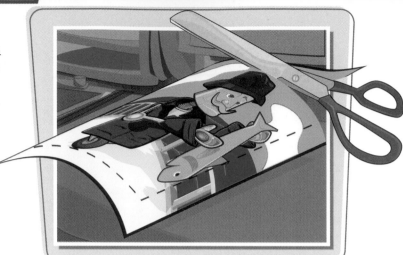

Improve Composition by Cropping

① Open a photo in the Quick Fix workspace.

② Click the **View** ⊡ and select **Before and After (Portrait)**.

③ Click the **Crop** tool (🔳).

    ⊹ changes to ✄.

④ Click the **Aspect Ratio** ⊡ and select **No Restriction**.

⑤ Click and drag in the after image and then release the mouse.

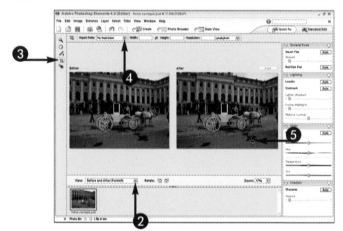

● A crop marquee appears as a box around the area of the photo to keep. The areas outside the crop are darkened.

● You can click and drag a corner handle of the marquee to adjust it.

● You can type a specific width and height in the data fields in the Options bar above the image.

⑥ Click inside the marquee to move it to another position.

● The marquee selection moves.

7 Click ✔ to apply the crop.

● You can click ⊘ to cancel the crop.

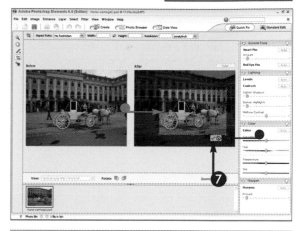

Elements crops the image.

Is there a quick way to crop to traditional photo sizes?

Yes. Click the **Aspect Ratio** ⌄, and you can select any of the options — such as 4 inches by 6 inches or 5 inches by 7 inches. You can invert the preset aspect ratio by clicking the **Swap** icon (⇄) to get a 6 inch by 4 inch crop or a 7 inch by 5 inch crop, for example.

Do I have to enter a number in the Resolution data field in the Options bar?

Not necessarily. When you use the **Crop** tool (▣) on a photo, the resolution remains the same as that of the original photo. For example, if your photo is 5 by 7 at 300ppi, and you crop the photo to 5 by 4 inches, the resolution of the new 5 by 4 inch photo remains set at 300ppi. If you click the **Aspect Ratio** ⌄ and choose a preset aspect ratio, the resolution automatically changes to match that of the preset.

Photoshop Elements includes many easy-to-use editing tools in the Quick Fix workspace. Depending on the image, the Quick Fix Auto buttons may be all you need to improve a photo. Because you can select a before and after view in the view area just below the image window, it is easy to see the results of each Auto button by comparing with the original photo.

Use Multiple Auto Buttons

You can apply one auto fix and then another. Although you can compound the effects of clicking the Auto buttons multiple times, you rarely need more than two or three to improve most photos. You can apply these in any order, with the exception of the Sharpen Auto Fix button, which should always be applied last.

Click and Slide to Adjust Photos

Clicking an Auto button makes the correction according to the software presets. You can make further edits or reduce the amount of the correction by using the sliders in each section. To apply the correction, click the **Commit** check mark, or click the **Cancel** icon to cancel the changes.

Auto Buttons Overview

The Smart Fix makes changes to the overall color balance in the photo including adjusting the highlights and shadows. It applies a more general correction. The Red Eye Fix automatically finds and removes red eye in the photo. The Auto Levels adjusts the contrast and the colors using the lightest and darkest pixels in the image, while the Auto Contrast only changes the contrast. The Auto Color fixes the contrast and color according to the highlights, midtones, and shadows. The Auto Sharpen sharpens the edges in the image using a default setting.

Try an Auto Fix for a Quick Improvement

Clicking any one or a combination of Quick Fix Auto buttons is a fast way to make general improvements to an image. If an Auto correction does not improve the photo, you can step backward by clicking Edit from the menu and selecting Undo. You can also start the editing all over again by clicking the Reset button above the after image.

Try an Auto Fix for a Quick Improvement

① Open a photo in the Quick Fix workspace.

② Click the **View** ▾ and select **Before and After (Portrait)**.

③ Click a **Quick Fix Auto** button; **Color** in this example.

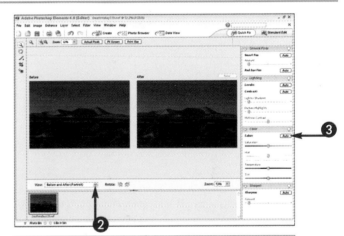

● The color and contrast of the after view change.

● You can click **Reset** if the change does not improve the photo.

You can repeat Step **3** using a different Auto button to find the appropriate correction.

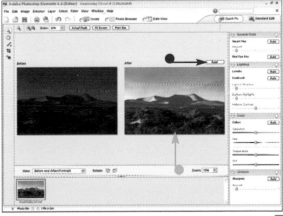

Remove Red Eye with One Click

Using a flash in a darkened room when the subject's pupils are enlarged often creates a red eye effect. Although many newer digital cameras can automatically remove red eye, Photoshop Elements includes a simple fix for this phenomenon.

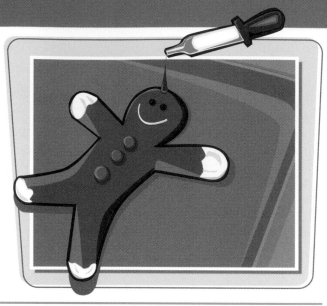

Remove Red Eye with One Click

① Open a photo in the Quick Fix workspace.

② Click the **View** ▾ and select **Before and After (Portrait)**.

③ Click the **Red Eye Fix Auto** button.

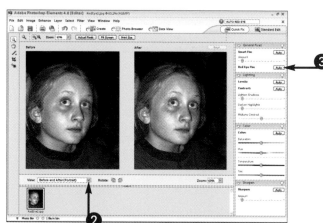

● The subject's red eye is automatically removed.

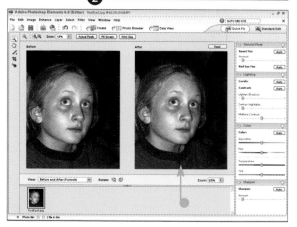

In the Quick Fix workspace, Photoshop Elements allows you to undo changes one step at a time using the Undo arrow in the Menu bar. You can also use the opposite arrow, or Redo arrow, to step forward again through your steps. The Reset button in the main image window erases all the steps at once, returning your image to its original state.

Undo Changes

① Open a photo in the Quick Fix workspace.

② Click the **View** 🔽 and select **Before and After (Portrait)**.

③ Click an **Auto Fix** button.

④ Click a second **Auto Fix** button.

⑤ Click another **Auto Fix** button or click and drag the sliders until you improve the photo to your liking.

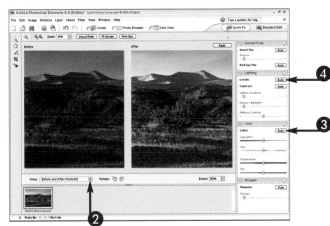

⑥ Click **Undo** (🔄) to undo a previous action.

⑦ Click **Redo** (🔄) to redo a previous action.

⑧ Click **Reset** to restore the original image.

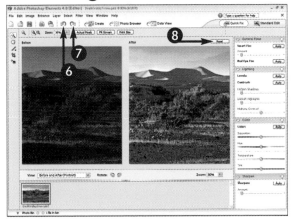

Convert a Color Photo to Black and White

You can easily change any color photograph to a black-and-white image, also called a grayscale image, using Photoshop Elements. Here is one quick way of making this conversion in the Quick Fix workspace.

Convert a Color Photo to Black and White

① Open a photo in the Quick Fix workspace.

② Click the **View** and select **Before and After (Portrait)**.

③ Click and drag the **Saturation** slider ( ) completely to the left.

The photo changes to black and white.

④ Click to apply the change.

● If the photo appears flat, you can click the **Auto Levels** button.

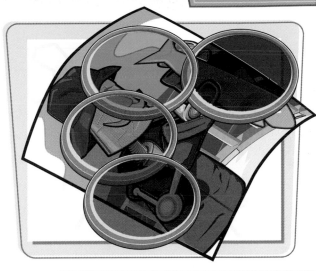

You can visually change the time of day or alter the entire mood of a photo by changing its overall color. By applying the digital equivalent of a colored lens filter in Photoshop Elements, you can repurpose any image, even a bland one, quickly and easily.

Add a Colored Filter Effect to Any Photo

① Open a photo in the Quick Fix workspace.

② Click the **View** ☑ and select **Before and After (Portrait)**.

③ Click and drag the **Saturation** slider completely to the left.

④ Click and drag the **Temperature** slider to the left to add a blue tone.

⑤ Click and drag the **Tint** slider to the right to add magenta for a purple tone.

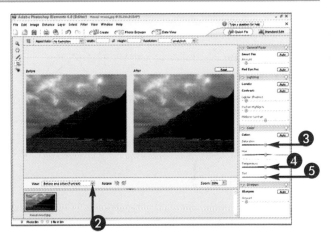

The image appears to have a purple filter applied.

⑥ Click ☑ to apply the changes.

Note: You can click and drag the **Temperature** slider to the right to add a red tone. You can click and drag the **Tint** slider to the left to add a green tone.

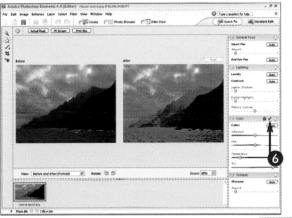

Enhancing Photos

Although the Quick Fix workspace allows you to make quick and easy edits to your photos, the Standard Edit workspace in Photoshop Elements offers a full line of powerful image editing tools. You can select the Standard Edit workspace from the Welcome screen or from within the Organizer. You can use the layers in this flexible workspace to adjust areas, crop with creative shapes, colorize, and more, and never alter your original image.

What Are Layers and Why Use Them?

A layer is like a sheet of glass over the main image or photo. Photoshop Elements uses different types of layers to help you improve your photos or completely change them without altering the original image. You can change the way each layer interacts with the layers below it by changing the layer's blend mode and the layer's opacity. Using layers is the key to digitally altering photos and creating various effects, including changing color and adding frames.

Duplicate the Background Layer

When you open a photo in the Editor workspace, you have one layer named Background in the **Layers** palette. It is a locked layer, meaning you cannot make certain types of changes to it. You can change the locked Background layer to an unlocked and editable layer by double-clicking the layer in the **Layers** palette and renaming the layer in the dialog box that appears. A preferable option is to create a duplicate of the Background layer by clicking **Layer** and then **Duplicate Layer**. Elements places a new identical but unlocked layer called Background copy above the Background in the **Layers** palette. You can then make changes to the duplicate, never risking the original, and you can delete the copy if you do not like your changes.

Add Other Image Layers

You can click and drag other open photos onto the Background image and Elements adds these as regular image layers. You can resize the individual image layer and make changes to the way it blends into or hides the image below. You can also add a new blank layer above the other photo layers by clicking the **Layer** menu and then **New** or by clicking the **Create a New Layer** icon (⬜) in the **Layers** palette.

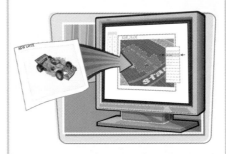

Add an Adjustment Layer

An Adjustment layer is a transparent overlay that allows you to make adjustments to the color and tones of the underlying layers. When you add an Adjustment layer, Elements places both a layer thumbnail and a layer mask thumbnail side by side in the **Layers** palette. You can add an Adjustment layer from the **Layer** menu or by clicking the **Adjustment Layer** icon (⬤) in the **Layers** palette.

About Layer Masks

Layer masks in Elements are attached to Adjustment or Fill layers and are used to hide or reveal areas of the image below the Adjustment layer. The mask starts out filled with white, making the adjustment cover the entire image below. You can remove parts of the mask and reveal portions of the underlying image by painting areas of the mask with black. Painting with darker or lighter shades of gray removes the mask in corresponding levels of transparency. Layer masks are often used to create composite images in which multiple photos blend into one another.

Add a Type Layer

When you select the **Type** tool ($\boxed{\text{T}}$) to add text to your photo, Elements places the text on a special kind of layer. You can edit the text, change the overall color, change the text direction, stylize, and warp the text on a Type layer. However, to add different colors to the individual letters or to apply filters to the text, you need to convert the Type layer into a normal image layer by clicking the **Layer** menu and selecting **Simplify Layer**. After it is simplified, you can no longer edit the text; however, the type can be blended into the photo in many ways.

Other Types of Layers

You can add Fill layers, which can contain a colored gradient, a solid color, or a pattern, and then blend the layer into the image using the layer blend mode or the layer opacity settings. You can also add Shape layers that are similar to Type layers and must be simplified so you can apply multiple colors or use filters on them.

Consolidate Multiple Layers

You can add as many layers as your computer's memory allows; however, layers increase the file size. You can *merge* some layers together to reduce the file size, and you can *flatten* all the layers when you are completely finished working on the image. Merging and flattening are permanent actions, and should be done only when you are finished editing the photo. You must flatten the layers to save the image for the Web or as an e-mail attachment.

Find Your Way Around the Layers Palette

The Layers palette is the key to working efficiently with layers in Photoshop Elements. The palette includes a thumbnail and the name of the layer. The icons and drop-down menus in the Layers palette allow you to make a variety of changes to the layers and to your overall image. You can access any of the commands that affect layers from Element's main menu; however, using the icons on the Layers palette is much quicker and easier.

Move the Layers Palette

All the layers for the open photo or image are listed in the **Layers** palette in the order in which they are added. You can move layers and change the order by clicking and dragging one layer above or below another layer in the **Layers** palette. Each time you add a layer, the list gets longer. You can extend the **Layers** palette by clicking and dragging on the bottom-right corner of the palette. Because it is so useful, you may want to drag the palette by its title tab out of the Palette Bin to make sure you can see all the layers on-screen. If you close the **Layers** palette, you can open it again from the main menu by clicking **Window** and then **Layers**.

Active Layers and Visibility

The layer you are currently working on is called the *active layer*. It is highlighted in blue. To make a change to the layer, such as applying a filter or erasing an area, you need to target and highlight the layer by clicking it. You cannot make certain types of changes to the original Background layer until you change it to a normal unlocked layer, as described in the previous section, "What Are Layers and Why Use Them?" You can hide or show a layer by clicking the **Visibility** icon (⬤) on and off. Hiding a layer is useful when you work on a duplicate and want to compare the before and after views with the original Background layer. Each time a new layer is added, you can use the default title for the layer or you can rename it to make it easier to identify. To rename a layer in the **Layers** palette, double-click its name and enter a new name in the highlighted title field.

The Layers Palette Icons

You can use the icons at the top of the Layers palette to apply many changes to the image quickly. Click the **Create a New Layer** icon (⬛) to add a new blank layer or click the **Create Adjustment Layer** icon (⬤) to add an adjustment or fill layer above the highlighted layer. If you click the **Delete Layer** icon (🗑), or trashcan, Elements immediately deletes the highlighted layer. You can link two or more layers together by pressing Shift and clicking all the layers you want to link. Then click the **Link Layers** icon (🔗). The Link icon appears on each linked layer. You can also protect a layer so it cannot be changed, moved, or deleted by highlighting the layer and clicking the **Lock All** icon (🔒). The **Lock Transparent Pixels** icon (🔲) is useful for protecting blank areas in a layer from being altered.

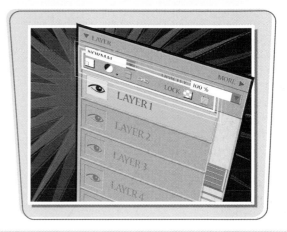

What Are Blending Modes and Opacity?

The Layers palette includes a drop-down menu for selecting the blend mode as well as the master opacity for each layer. The blend mode determines how the pixels on that layer affect the pixels in the layer below. In Normal mode, whatever is on that layer acts as a completely new image and blocks the layer below. The other blend modes are grouped in the list by the way they interact with the layer below, for example, darkening or lightening the image. Click the **Opacity** arrow (▶) to use the slider to adjust the opacity of the layer or enter the numbers for the percentage directly in the data field. You can even click and drag directly on the word Opacity to activate the scrubby sliders, which change the layer opacity as you move the cursor.

There Is More!

You can click the **More** ▶ at the top right of the **Layers** palette to access all the other commands for layers also found in the main **Layer** menu. From this drop-down menu you can add, delete, rename, and link layers. In addition, you can choose **Merge Down**, which merges the highlighted layer with the layer below; **Merge Visible**, which merges all the layers that are currently visible; and **Flatten Image**, which merges all the visible layers and deletes any hidden layers. You can also choose **Simplify a Type or Shape layer** and even change the thumbnail size when you choose **Palette Options**.

Straighten a Crooked Photo

You may have photos where the horizon is not quite level or a vertical building is leaning over. Photoshop Elements 4 includes a new Straighten tool to help you align the horizon or adjust a vertical line. You can even have Elements automatically remove the blank background areas that are created when straightening an image.

Straighten a Crooked Photo

STRAIGHTEN A HORIZON

1 Open a photo in the Standard Edit workspace.

2 Click the **Straighten** tool (▦).

3 Select **Rotate All Layers** (☐ changes to ☑).

4 Click the **Canvas Options** ☑ and select **Crop to Remove Background**.

5 Click and drag along the horizon line in the photo and then release the mouse.

The photo is straightened and cropped to remove any blank background.

STRAIGHTEN A VERTICAL BUILDING

1 Open a photo in the Standard Edit workspace.

2 Click the **Straighten** tool ().

3 Select **Rotate All Layers** (changes to).

4 Click the **Canvas Options** and select **Crop to Remove Background**.

5 Press and hold Ctrl as you click and drag along a vertical line in the photo and then release the mouse.

The photo is straightened and cropped to remove any blank background.

TIPS

Are there any other choices for the background?

Yes. When you click the **Canvas Options** , you can also select **Grow Canvas to Fit**, which enlarges the canvas to fit the rotated image. This selection shows the blank areas of the background where it was rotated but includes the entire original photo. You can also select **Crop to Original Size**. In this case, the cropped photo appears straightened on a blank background exactly the same size as the original image, but the corners are cut off.

How do I make my photo open on a gray background as in the examples?

You can view your photo as a photo file with a gray background by clicking the **Maximize Mode** icon () in the title bar of the image or the same icon in the main menu bar in Photoshop Elements.

Add a Quick Colored Matte

You can use Photoshop Element's Crop tool to add a white or colored matte to any photo. You can set the background color in the toolbar to any color for your matte and then use the Crop tool to create a reverse crop and make the canvas larger than the original photo. This technique is useful to visually preview your photo on a colored background or for off-setting the photo for a greeting card.

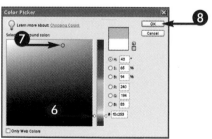

Add a Quick Colored Matte

① Open a photo in the Standard Edit workspace.

② Click the **Zoom** tool (🔍).

③ Click the **Zoom out** option (🔍) in the Options bar.

④ Click the photo to zoom out.

● This leaves a wide gray border around the photo.

⑤ Click the **Background** color.

The Color Picker appears.

⑥ Click and drag the slider to select a color range.

⑦ Click in the color field to select the color.

⑧ Click **OK**.

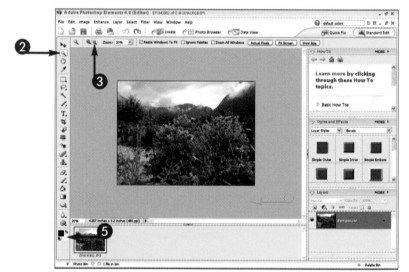

● The background color is set to the new color.

9 Click the **Crop** tool (⬚).

10 Click and drag across the entire photo.

11 Click and drag each of the four corners of the Crop marquee to increase the size.

12 Click the **Commit Crop** button (✓).

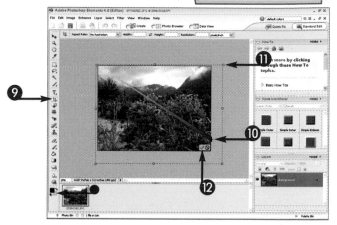

The photo appears on a large colored matte.

Note: *You determine the proportions of the colored matte visually when you drag the corners of the Crop marquee. To create a matte with exact proportions, see the task "Frame a Photo with a Background Layer," later in this chapter.*

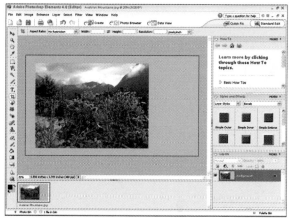

TIPS

Is there a quick way to make a white matte?

Yes. Instead of clicking the **Background** color to open the Color Picker, click the small default color boxes (⬛) to set white as the background color automatically. Then continue with Steps **9** to **12** to reverse crop the photo and create a white matte.

Can I make a black matte?

Yes. First click the small default color boxes (⬛) to set the default colors to a black foreground and a white background. Then click the **Switch Default Colors** arrow (�)). You can also use the keyboard shortcuts. Press **D** to set the default colors and **X** to switch them.

Make a Creative Crop

Photoshop Elements includes a Cookie Cutter tool to help you crop your photos into unique shapes. Although the default set of shapes is limited, the application includes more than 500 shapes, which you can load into the Custom Shape Picker. Turn your photos into various shapes or give them a custom brushed edge by cropping them with the Cookie Cutter.

Make a Creative Crop

LOAD SHAPES INTO THE CUSTOM SHAPE PICKER

① Open a photo in the Standard Edit workspace.

② Click the **Cookie Cutter** tool ( ).

③ Click the **Shape** ▾ in the Options bar.

The Custom Shape Picker opens.

You can choose a shape from what is visible in the Picker.

④ Click ▸ to open the pop-up palette.

⑤ Click **All Elements Shapes**.

Elements loads additional shapes into the Custom Shape Picker.

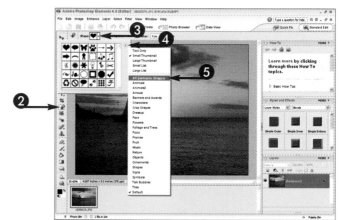

CROP THE PHOTO

⑥ Scroll through the Custom Shape Picker and double-click a shape thumbnail.

⑦ Click and drag in the image to create the shape.

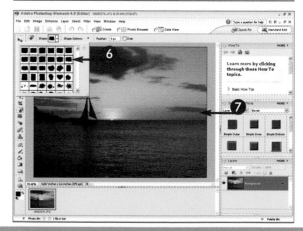

The photo is cut out to fit the shape on a transparent background.

● You can click and drag the handles to resize the shape to better fit the photo.

⑧ Click the **Commit** button ().

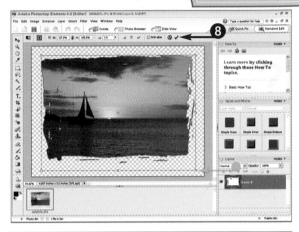

The photo is cropped to the unique shape.

● The Background layer is automatically changed to Layer 0.

TIP

How can I change the checkerboard background?

The checkerboard indicates transparent areas on the layer. Create a new layer by clicking the **Create a New Layer** icon (▣) in the **Layers** palette. Then in the **Layers** palette, click the new layer and drag it below the photo layer. Click **Edit** and then **Fill Layer**. The Fill Layer dialog box appears. Click the **Use** ▾ and select white, black, or a color. The background fills with white or the chosen color. To finish the creatively cropped photo, combine the two layers into one by clicking **Layer** and then **Flatten Image**.

Select an Area of a Photo

You can edit and adjust a specific area of a photo, such as a person's teeth or the petals of a flower, by making a selection. You can use the new Magic Selection Brush tool to scribble on an area. Photoshop Elements then makes the selection based on the color and texture of the scribbled area. You can add to or remove areas from the selection using the Indicate Foreground and Indicate Background brushes in the Options bar.

Select an Area of a Photo

① Open a photo in the Standard Edit workspace.

② Click the **Zoom** tool (🔍).

③ Click and drag across the selection area to zoom in.

④ Click the **Magic Selection Brush** (✎).

Note: An explanation dialog box appears. Click **OK** to close the dialog box or click **Don't show again** (☐ changes to ☑), so that selecting the tool does not open the dialog box each time.

⑤ Click and drag to scribble over the area to select.

Note: A red scribble appears temporarily on the photo.

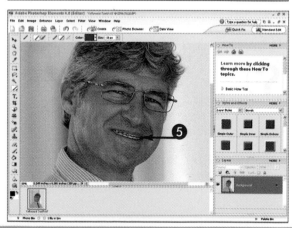

A selection border appears around the area.

6 Click the **Indicate Foreground** tool (■) in the Options bar.

7 Click and drag to scribble in red over any areas to be added to the selection.

8 Click the **Indicate Background** tool (■) in the Options bar.

9 Click and drag to scribble in blue over any areas to be removed from the selection.

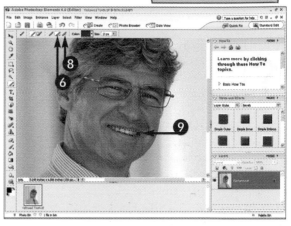

10 Repeat Steps **6** to **9** if necessary.

● A selection border only appears around the desired area.

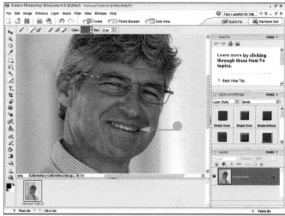

Are there other ways to make selections?

Yes. You can use the **Rectangular Marquee** tool (■) or the **Elliptical Marquee** tool (■) to select those shapes. You can use the **Lasso** tool (■) to freely draw any shape, the **Polygonal Lasso** tool (■) to draw a straight-edged shape, and the **Magnetic Lasso** tool (■) to select an area with strong contrast to the background. You can use the **Magic Wand** tool (■) to select pixels within the same color range, and the **Selection Brush** tool (■) to paint a selection directly on an area.

Can I save a selection to make more changes?

Yes. After your selection has a selection border, click **Select** and then **Save Selection**. The Save Selection dialog box appears. Type a name for the new selection in the **Name** box, make sure the ■ for **New Selection** is filled, and click **OK**. To edit the selected area, click **Select** and then **Load Selection**. Find the name of the selection and click **OK** to load the selection marquee on the photo.

Whiten Teeth Digitally

You can quickly improve any portrait photo by lightening the teeth of a smiling subject. This three-step technique involves making a selection, removing the yellow, and lightening the teeth. Be careful to not make the teeth too white and the enhancement unrealistic.

Whiten Teeth Digitally

① Follow the steps in the previous task, "Select an Area of a Photo," to make a selection of the teeth.

② Click **Select**.

③ Click **Feather**.

The Feather Selection dialog box appears.

④ Type a value in pixels in the **Feather Radius** box; for example, type **1** to feather the selection by 1 pixel.

⑤ Click **OK**.

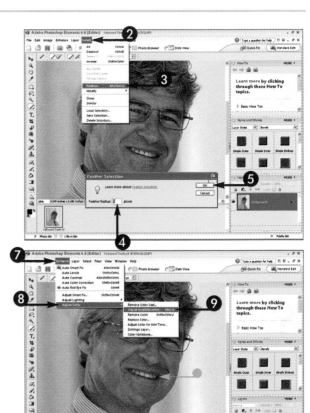

⑥ Press Ctrl + H to hide the selection marquee.

Note: Hiding the marquee makes it easier to judge the color as you adjust it.

● The teeth remain selected, but the selection marquee is not visible.

Note: This is a totally visual technique. You should zoom out to view a large area of the photo before you make adjustments.

⑦ Click **Enhance**.

⑧ Click **Adjust Color**.

⑨ Click **Adjust Hue/Saturation**.

The Hue/Saturation dialog box appears.

Note: Move the dialog box, if necessary, to see the selected area.

⑩ Click the **Edit** ▾ and select **Yellows**.

⑪ Click and drag the **Saturation** slider to the left until there is no visible yellow in the teeth.

● The teeth will have a slight gray tone.

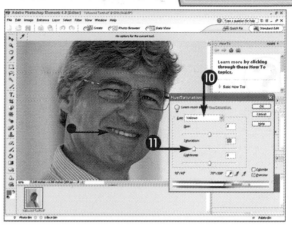

⑫ Click the **Edit** ▾ and select **Master**.

⑬ Click and drag the **Lightness** slider to the right until the teeth appear whitened but still natural.

⑭ Click **OK**.

⑮ Press Ctrl + D to deselect the teeth.

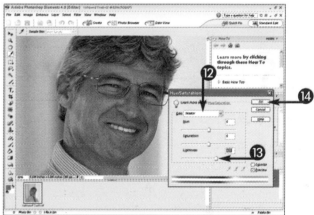
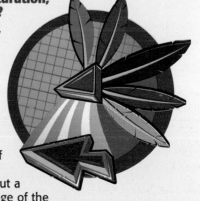

TIPS

What does feathering the selection do?	**To what do Hue, Saturation, and Lightness refer?**
Feathering a selection creates a soft transition between the selection and the surrounding area by blurring the edges. By softening the edges, the colors blend smoothly and the enhancement appears more natural. To feather the selection of teeth in a portrait, a feather of 1 to 2 pixels is generally sufficient.	Hue is the actual color, such as red or green, and Saturation is the intensity or purity of the color. The **Lightness** slider controls the lightness or tonal range of the color and works with the other two sliders. If you change the **Lightness** slider without a selection, the tonal range of the entire photo is affected.

What Are Photoshop Elements Filters?

The numerous filters included in Photoshop Elements help you retouch or enhance your photos in different ways. Filters allow you to make specific improvements, such as reducing the noise in an image or changing the lighting, as well as making a totally new image out of the original photo. You can apply a filter to the entire photo or to a selection on a photo.

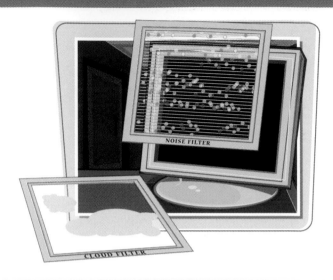

Use Photoshop Elements Filters on Separate Layers

By applying a filter to a duplicate of the original Background layer, or to a selection placed on a separate layer, you can alter your photo and never alter the original. You can use a duplicate layer to make it easy to compare the effect on the photo by clicking the **Visibility** icon ( ) for the filtered layer on and off in the **Layers** palette. If you do not like the changes, you can quickly undo them by dragging the filtered layer to the **Layers** palette trashcan ( ).

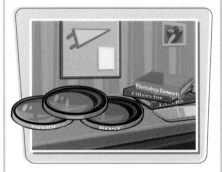

Types of Photoshop Elements Filters

Photoshop Elements includes a wide variety of filters grouped into various categories according to the effect that is created. Other software companies, such as nik multimedia, Inc., make filters that you can install in Photoshop Elements. After they are installed, the added filters appear at the bottom of the Filter menu. These third-party filters often make better improvements or help you make photo corrections more easily.

Adjustment Filters and Adjustment Layer Options

Some filters can be applied as an Adjustment layer, a special layer that floats over the photo layer and alters the colors or tones of the image underneath. When you apply a filter as an Adjustment layer, you select it from the **Layer** menu rather than the **Filter** menu. Unlike a filter from the **Filter** menu, which only affects one layer, a filter applied as an Adjustment layer affects all the layers below it in the **Layers** palette.

Duplicating the Background layer is a safety step in correcting digital photos. By applying filters or making other alterations to the Background copy layer, your original photo remains untouched. You can easily compare the before and after images by clicking the Visibility icon on and off next to the Background copy layer. You can also quickly delete the Background copy layer to revert to the original photo.

Duplicate the Background Layer

① Open a photo in the Standard Edit workspace.

② Click **Layer**.

③ Click **Duplicate Layer**.

The Duplicate Layer dialog box appears.

● You can accept the default duplicate layer name, Background copy, or you can type another name.

④ Click **OK**.

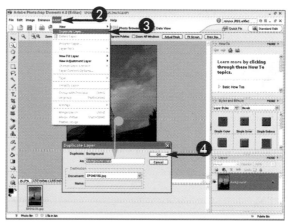

● The Background copy layer is placed above the Background layer in the Layers palette.

● You can click and drag the Background layer over the **Create a New Layer** icon (🔲) at the top of the **Layers** palette instead of using the **Layer** menu. When you release the mouse, the duplicate Background layer is automatically created and given the default name.

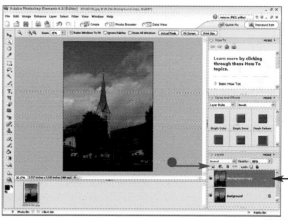

Reduce Digital Noise

Many photos show stray pixels of color or appear grainy. Such digital noise is most apparent in photos shot without a flash in low light conditions or at high ISO settings. (See Chapter 4 for more about ISO settings.) You can reduce the amount of such unwanted artifacts by applying the Reduce Noise filter in Photoshop Elements.

Reduce Digital Noise

① Open a photo in the Standard Edit workspace and duplicate the Background layer as described in the previous task, "Duplicate the Background Layer."

② Click **Filter**.

③ Click **Noise**.

④ Click **Reduce Noise**.

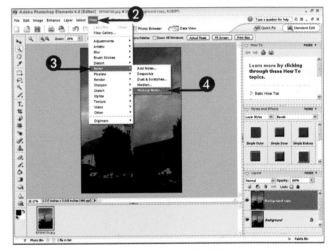

The Reduce Noise dialog box appears.

⑤ Click ⊞ to enlarge the preview area.

⑥ Click in the preview area and drag to see both detail and noise areas.

Note: *Because noise is more visible in large areas of color such as the sky, you need to view some of the detail areas, such as the steeple in the example, as you apply the filter to make sure you do not blur edges or lose details in the photo.*

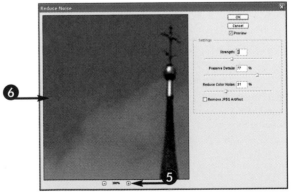

7 Click and drag the **Strength** slider to the right slowly to reduce the overall noise.

8 Click and drag the **Preserve Details** slider to the right to limit the blurring effect created when reducing noise.

9 Click and drag the **Reduce Color Noise** slider to the right to reduce the amount of extraneous color specs in the photo.

10 Click **Remove JPEG Artifact** (changes to ✓) to remove the white halos and white artifacts around contrasting areas.

11 Click **OK**.

The filter is applied to the Background copy layer.

12 Click the **Zoom** tool ( ).

13 Click **Actual Pixels** to view at 100 percent.

The photo shows fewer artifacts and smoother areas of color.

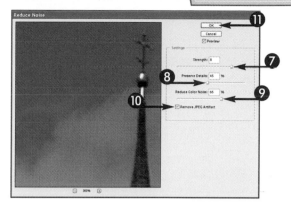

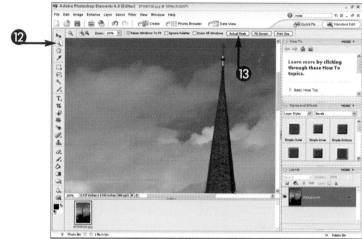

What does the Remove JPEG Artifact check box do?

JPEG artifacts are lighter colored pixels or halos that are created every time an image is saved as a JPEG. Selecting **Remove JPEG Artifact** generally lessens these undesirable blocks and halos in the photo.

Why is there more noise in the photo when I click in the Preview window to move the image around?

Clicking and holding the mouse in the Preview window shows the photo before the noise filter is applied. This is a quick way to see the before and after views, even before you apply the filter.

Use Special Effect Lighting

You can change the overall lighting in the photo and even simulate studio lighting after the photo has been shot using the Lighting Effects filter included in Photoshop Elements. You can focus attention on a specific area of the image or concentrate on the main subject, or completely change the mood of the photo with the type of lighting effect you apply.

Use Special Effect Lighting

① Open a photo in the Standard Edit workspace and duplicate the Background layer as described in the task "Duplicate the Background Layer," earlier in this chapter.

② Click **Filter**.

③ Click **Render**.

④ Click **Lighting Effects**.

The Lighting Effects dialog box appears.

⑤ Click the **Style** ⮟ and select a lighting style.

⑥ Click the **Light type** ⮟ and select the type of light to use.

7 Click and drag the handles to adjust the shape and size of the light.

8 Click and drag the center handle to move the light over the main focus.

9 Click **OK**.

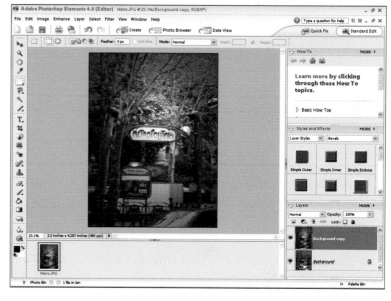

Photoshop Elements applies the lighting effect to the photo.

Can I save a special lighting style to apply it to multiple photos?

Yes. You can create a special lighting style using any sliders and options you want. To save the style, click **Save** in the Lighting Effects dialog box. In the dialog box that appears, type a name for the style and click **OK**. Your new lighting style appears in the Lighting Effects dialog box **Style** menu.

What do the Properties options do?

The sliders under the Properties section of the dialog box give you options to control how the light reflects from the surface of the photo using the **Gloss** slider or from the object on which the light is cast using the **Material** slider. You can also control how much light is applied using the **Exposure** slider and whether the new light source is pure or mixed with the ambient light with the **Ambience** slider.

Liquify a Photo for Effect

The Liquify filter in Photoshop Elements allows you to move pixels in the photo as if you were sculpting clay. You can push, pull, pucker, or bloat pixels and more. You can use this filter to correct shapes of objects and people, or to completely exaggerate items for effect.

Liquify a Photo for Effect

① Open a photo in the Standard Edit workspace and duplicate the Background layer as described in the task "Duplicate the Background Layer," earlier in this chapter.

② Click **Filter**.

③ Click **Distort**.

④ Click **Liquify**.

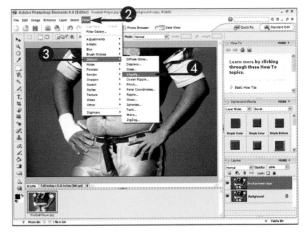

The Liquify dialog box appears.

⑤ Click the **Warp** tool (🖐).

⑥ Click the **Brush Size** ▶.

⑦ Move the slider to adjust the brush size.

⑧ Click and drag in the photo to move the pixels.

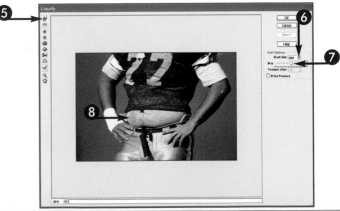

⑨ Click the **Pucker** tool (🖼️) to squeeze areas.

⑩ Click the **Bloat** tool (🔷) to enlarge areas.

⑪ Click **OK**.

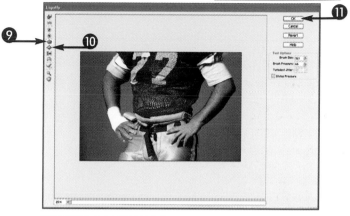

Photoshop Elements applies the changes to the photo.

How do I determine the brush size?
The brush size depends on the area of the image you are adjusting. You want the brush size to be larger than the area you are moving to avoid a rippled appearance.

What if I liquify too much?
You can move pixels slowly back and more toward their original position by clicking the **Reconstruct** tool (🖌️) and using it to click and drag on the area. You can also click **Revert** to completely remove all the changes at once.

Add Motion Blur

When you set an exposure time to take a photo of a moving object, or when you pan to take the photo, the objects in the photo appear to be moving because some areas are blurred. You can add this effect in Photoshop Elements using the Motion Blur filter and even control the direction and angle of the blur. By adding the motion blur to a duplicate layer, you can erase parts of that layer allowing the original image to show in areas that do not have motion.

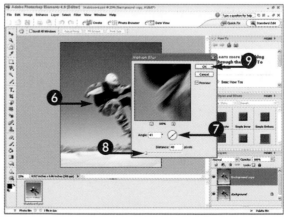

Add Motion Blur

① Open a photo in the Standard Edit workspace and duplicate the Background layer as described in the task "Duplicate the Background Layer," earlier in this chapter.

② Click the **Background copy** layer in the Layers palette to select it.

③ Click **Filter**.

④ Click **Blur**.

⑤ Click **Motion Blur**.

The Motion Blur dialog box appears.

⑥ Click in the preview image to move to an area to view.

⑦ Click and drag here to direct the angle to match the photo.

⑧ Click and drag the **Distance** slider to indicate the amount of motion.

⑨ Click **OK**.

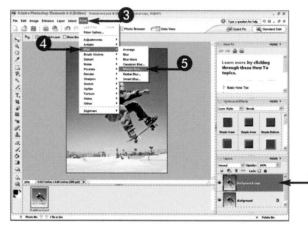

Photoshop Elements applies the motion blur to the entire photo layer.

⑩ Click the **Eraser** tool (🗹).

⑪ Click ⏷ to open the Brush presets.

⑫ Click a large soft-edged brush to select it.

⑬ Click and drag to erase the areas of the photo that should not show motion.

Photoshop Elements erases those areas on the Background copy layer, allowing the unchanged parts of the original background photo to show through.

TIPS

What is a large soft-edged brush?

You can select various types of brushes in the Brush preset list. The soft-edged brushes are the ones that show fuzzy edges in the thumbnail. You can use the soft-edged brushes when you want the parts of the photo to blend into one another smoothly.

When do I use the other types of blur filters?

Click **Filter** and then **Blur** for other blur filters. You can select the **Gaussian Blur** to produce a soft focus effect, the **Radial Blur** to simulate a rotating camera, and the **Blur** and **Blur More** filters to smooth any color changes or transitions in the photo. You can use the **Smart Blur** filter to precisely control the amount and distance of a camera blur and create depth of field digitally.

Colorize a
Black-and-White Photo

You can make any black-and-white photo appear hand-colored using a separate layer and the Soft Light layer Blending mode. You can select the colors for different areas and hand color the entire photo, or only color specific areas for effect.

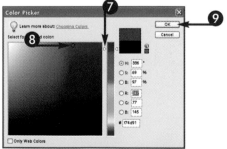

① Open a photo in the Standard Edit workspace and duplicate the Background layer as described in the task "Duplicate the Background Layer," earlier in this chapter.

② Click the **Create a New Layer** icon (⬜) to add a new blank layer above the Background copy layer.

③ Click ⬇.

④ Click **Soft Light** from the menu that appears.

⑤ Click the **Brush** tool (🖌).

⑥ Click the **Foreground** color.

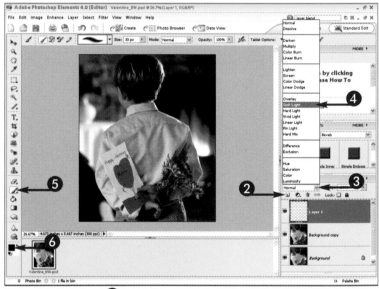

The Color Picker appears.

⑦ Click and drag the slider to select a color range.

⑧ Click in the color field to select a color.

⑨ Click **OK**.

⑩ Click ▾ to open the Brush presets.

⑪ Click a small soft-edged brush to select it.

⑫ Click and drag over an area to paint in the color.

Note: Press `Ctrl` + `Spacebar` to temporarily use the **Zoom in** tool and drag across the area to zoom in, if necessary. Press `Spacebar` to temporarily use the **Hand** tool to move around in the enlarged photo.

⑬ Repeat Steps **5** to **12** for each area you want to color.

Note: Repeat Steps **10** and **11** to select a different brush size, if necessary.

⑭ Click the **Opacity** ▸.

⑮ Move the slider to the left to lower the strength of the colors.

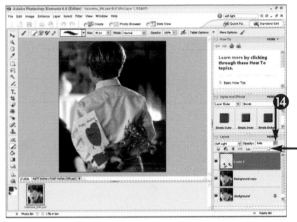

TIPS

What does the Soft Light Blending mode do?

The Layer Blending modes determine how the pixels on the top layer blend with the pixels in the layer below. The Soft Light Blending mode applies the new color to the gray tones in the black-and-white photo, without changing the lightness values of the pixels. The colors appear as a colored veil over the image.

Is there a faster way to change brush size?

Yes. With the **Brush** tool (✐) selected, you can press the **Right Bracket** key (▯) on the keyboard to increase the brush size and the **Left Bracket** key (▯) to reduce brush size.

Create a Sepia-Toned Photo

You can create an "old style" sepia-toned photo from any color or black-and-white image using Photoshop Elements. You can add an Adjustment layer with a brown color as the foreground color and change the Layer Blending mode to blend the sepia with the image on the layer below. You can even change the color of the sepia at any time to suit your taste.

Create a Sepia-Toned Photo

CHANGE THE FOREGROUND COLOR

1. Open a photo in the Standard Edit workspace.

2. Click the **Foreground** color.

   The Color Picker appears.

3. Click and drag the slider to select the brown color range.

4. Click in the color field to select a sepia brown color.

5. Click **OK**.

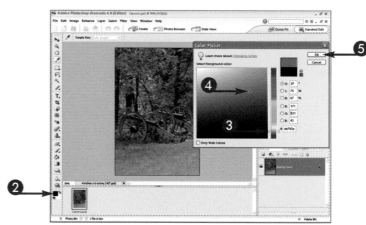

6. Click **Layer**.

7. Click **New Adjustment Layer**.

8. Click **Gradient Map**.

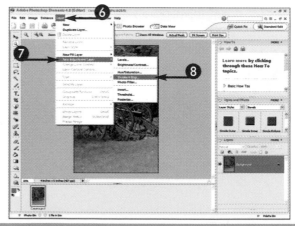

The New Layer dialog box opens.

9 Click the **Mode** ⏷.

10 Select **Color** from the menu that appears.

11 Click **OK** to close the New Layer dialog box.

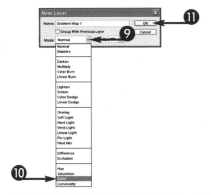

A Sepia tone Gradient Map Adjustment layer is applied to the image.

The Gradient Map dialog box opens.

12 Click **OK** to close the dialog box.

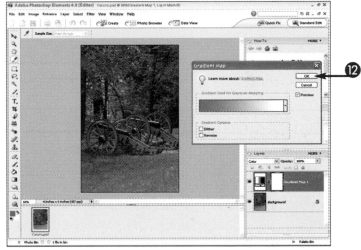

Why use an Adjustment layer?

An Adjustment layer allows you to change colors and tones in an image without changing the original image. You can use multiple adjustment layers and delete any or all of them without affecting the original photo. You can also change the tonal and color adjustments any number of times without changing the original photo.

How do I choose a different color after the Adjustment layer is applied?

Depending on your photo and your personal preference, you can select a different shade for the sepia-toned photo, or change it to another color altogether, even after applying the Gradient Map. Double-click the **Gradient Map** thumbnail in the **Layers** palette. The Gradient Map dialog box appears. Click inside the gradient in the Gradient Map dialog box to bring up the Gradient Editor. Double-click the sepia **Color Stop** to open the Color Picker. Click another color in the color field and then click **OK**. Click **OK** to close the Gradient Editor, and again to close the Gradient Map dialog box.

Understanding Styles and Effects

Photoshop Elements includes not only numerous filters to help you alter or enhance your photos, but it also has many effects and layer styles. These special effects and preconfigured layer styles are found in the Styles and Effects palette, so you can apply them with a click of the mouse.

What Are Layer Styles?

Layer styles apply a predesigned image style to the entire layer. The style is nondestructive, meaning it acts as an adjustment layer and does not permanently change the pixels in the original image. Styles affect the layer's content. If you change what is on the layer, the style is applied to the new content.

Different Types of Layer Styles

Layer styles include Bevels, Shadows, and Glows, which give borders to the layer. Other layer styles, such as Glass Buttons, Patterns, and the Wow libraries, totally cover the entire layer.

Create Custom Styles

Layer styles are cumulative. You can continue to click the Style thumbnails in the Styles and Effects palette to add one style onto another creating an original style. You can edit the attributes of certain styles by double-clicking the *f* icon (⦿) on the layer. You can then move the sliders in the dialog box that appears to edit the style.

Remove Styles Quickly

You can remove all the layer styles applied to an individual layer by clicking the **Layer** menu and selecting **Layer Style** and then **Clear Layer Style**. However, you can also click and drag the **f** icon (🖉) on the layer over the **Layers** palette trashcan (🗑) and release the mouse.

Apply and Remove Effects

Unlike layer styles, which are applied by clicking once on the thumbnail in the Styles and Effects palette, you can apply an effect by doubling-clicking its thumbnail. To remove an effect, click the **Undo** arrow (🔁) in the Options bar. If the effect is on a separate layer, you can click and drag that layer to the **Layers** palette trashcan (🗑).

What Are Effects?

Effects are actually a series of steps that are programmed to give a specific look to the image. Although effects include filters, layer styles, and other functions, you only click and see the resulting effect. Some effects can only be applied to a selection on a layer or to type. Others require the layers to be flattened or combined as they can only work on the Background layer. Still other effects automatically create a duplicate layer and apply the effect to that layer. Effects include Frames, Image Effects, Text Effects, and Textures.

Effects and Memory

Effects like filters use a lot of your computer's memory (RAM) to create and apply changes to photos. The larger the photo file you are working on, the more memory is required to apply effects and filters. To free up as much memory as possible so Photoshop Elements can function efficiently, you should exit from other applications. You can also make more memory available by clicking **Edit**, **Clear**, and then **All** to clear the undo history and Clipboard within Photoshop Elements.

Customize the Palette View

In addition to the Layers palette, the Styles and Effects palette makes it easy to use all the image editing power of Photoshop Elements. From this palette, you can not only apply the various layer styles and effects, but also access almost all the filters listed in the Filters menu. Customizing the Palette view can make you much more productive.

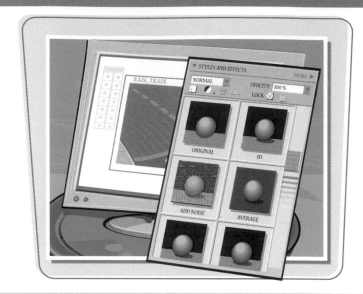

① Click ☑ to close the **How To** palette.

● The Styles and Effects palette automatically moves up in the palette bin.

② Click the **Layers** palette **More** ▶.

③ Select **Palette Options**.

The Layers Palette Options dialog box appears. You can change several Layers palette settings in this dialog box.

④ Click the smallest thumbnail size (○ changes to ◉).

⑤ Click **OK**.

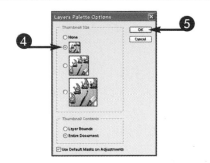

● The **Layers** palette thumbnails become smaller, so more layers can fit in the palette.

● You can also click the **Styles and Effects** palette's **More** ▶ and select **List View** to see the choices as a list rather than as large thumbnails.

TIP

How can I see all the different types of styles and effects?
Click the left ▾ on the **Styles and Effects** palette. Select a category: **Effects**, **Filters**, or **Layer Styles**. Then click the right ▾ on the **Styles and Effects** palette to view a library menu. You can select **All** from the Effects or Filters categories to see all the choices at once or select a specific type from the menu. You cannot view all the layer styles at once. You can select and view a particular layer styles library such as Bevels or Drop Shadows.

Add a Quick Vignette

A vignette gives any photo a traditional look. You can easily add a vignette by first making a selection of the main focus of the photo and applying an effect from the Styles and Effects menu.

Add a Quick Vignette

① Open a photo in the Standard Edit workspace.

② Click the **Rectangular Marquee** tool (▢).

③ Click the **Elliptical Marquee** tool (⬭).

④ Click and drag an ellipse around the main subject.

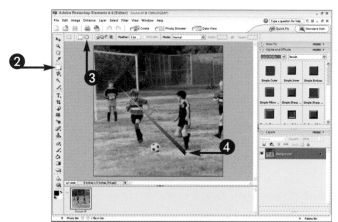

⑤ Click ▼ and select **Effects**.

⑥ Click ▼ and select **frames**.

⑦ Scroll down the list and double-click the **Vignette (selection)** thumbnail.

● Photoshop Elements creates a new white layer and places the vignette on the top layer.

TIPS

Can I create a vignette with a different shape?

Yes. You can select a rectangle or square using the **Rectangular Marquee** tool (⬚) or you can make any shape selection with one of the **Lasso** tools (𝒫).

How do I change the white background to a different color?

Click the white layer to highlight it. Click **Edit** and select **Fill Layer**. In the Fill Layer dialog box that appears, click the **Use** ☑ and select **Black** or **50% Gray**, or select **Color** to choose a color from the Color Picker.

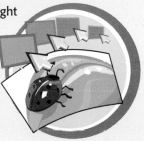

Add Digital Photo Corners

Photoshop Elements includes a variety of photo frame styles in the Effects category of the Styles and Effects palette. Try applying digital photo corners to make any image look as though it came from a traditional photo album.

Add Digital Photo Corners

① Open a photo in the Standard Edit workspace.

② Click ▾ and select **Effects**.

③ Click ▾ and select **frames**.

④ Double-click **Photo Corners**.

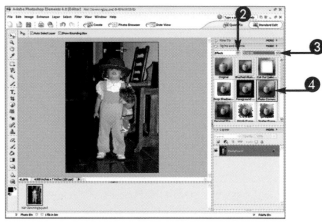

Photoshop Elements applies the photo corners to the photo on a new layer.

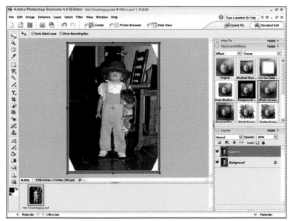

Turn a Photo into a Drawing

You can use the Image Effects library from the Effects category of the Styles and Effects palette to quickly turn an ordinary photo into a stylized drawing without any drawing skills.

Turn a Photo into a Drawing

① Open a photo in the Standard Edit workspace.

② Click ☑ and select **Effects**.

③ Click ☑ and select **image effects**.

④ Double-click **Fluorescent Chalk**.

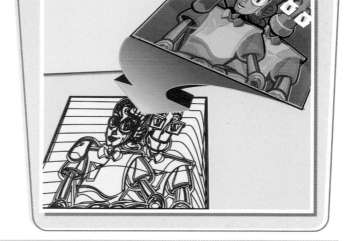

Photoshop Elements applies the image effect to the photo.

Frame a Photo with a Background Layer

You can use layers and the Styles and Effects palette in Photoshop Elements to give any photo a finished look by placing it on a new background. Add drop shadows or bevels to create the illusion of a frame or to just add depth to the overall image.

Frame a Photo with a Background Layer

CHANGE THE BACKGROUND LAYER TO A REGULAR LAYER

① Open a photo in the Standard Edit workspace.

② Double-click the **Background** layer in the Layers palette.

The New Layer dialog box appears.

● You can accept the default layer name, Layer 0, or you can type another name.

③ Click **OK**.

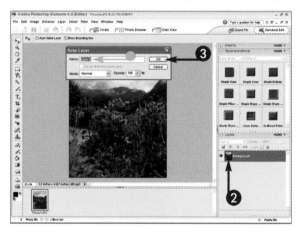

The Background layer name changes to Layer 0.

④ Click the **Create a New Layer** icon (▣) to add a new blank layer.

⑤ Click and drag the new layer labeled Layer 1 below Layer 0 in the **Layers** palette.

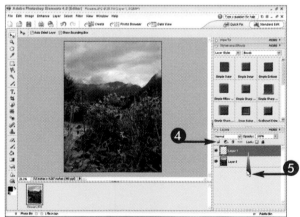

INCREASE THE CANVAS SIZE

● Make sure the blank layer, Layer 1, is highlighted.

6 Click **Image**.

7 Click **Resize**.

8 Click **Canvas Size**.

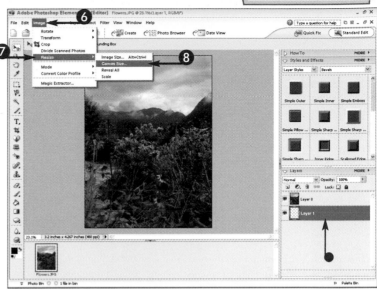

The Canvas Size dialog box appears.

9 Select **Relative** (☐ changes to ☑).

10 Type an amount in the **Width** and **Height** data fields.

Note: The number you type represents the increased area around the photo.

11 Click **OK**.

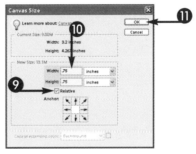

How can I add a simple black outline to the photo?
Press **Ctrl** and click directly on the photo thumbnail in the **Layers** palette to select it. The selection marquee appears around the photo. Then click **Edit** and **Stroke (Outline) Selection**. The Stroke dialog box appears. If necessary, click the **Color** box to open the Color Picker and set the color to black. Type a number in the **Width** data field. Click **Outside** (○ changes to ●) and click **OK**. The black outline stroke is added to the photo layer. Click **Ctrl** + **D** to remove the selection marquee.

continued

Because the Photo layer is separate from the background, you can easily create many different looks with the same photo. You can have one version on a white background with a beveled edge, another on a colored background with a drop shadow, and even a version with a simple black line around the photo.

Frame a Photo with a Background Layer *(continued)*

FILL THE NEW BACKGROUND WITH WHITE

The photo is now on a larger empty background.

⑫ Click **Edit**.

⑬ Select **Fill Layer**.

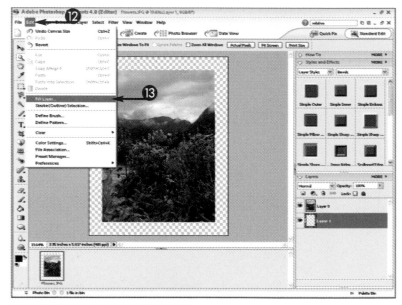

The Fill Layer dialog box appears.

⑭ Click the **Use** ⬇ and select **White**.

⑮ Click **OK**.

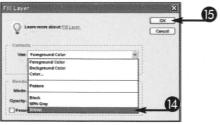

ADD A LAYER STYLE TO THE PHOTO

The new background called Layer 1 fills with white.

⑯ Click the photo layer, Layer 0, to highlight it.

⑰ Click ☑ and select **Layer Styles**.

⑱ Click ☑ and select **Bevels**.

⑲ Click a bevel thumbnail to apply it.

The bevel is applied to the photo making it stand out on the background.

TIPS

How can I add a colored background?

In the **Fill Layer** dialog box, you can click the **Use** ☑ and select **Color** instead of **White**. The Color Picker appears, and you can select a specific color for the background.

Can I add a drop shadow and a bevel to the photo?

Yes. In the **Styles and Effects** palette, after you click ☑ and choose **Layer Styles**, you can click ☑ and select the **Drop Shadow** library. You can click a drop shadow thumbnail before or after you click a bevel. The layer styles are cumulative.

Remove Blemishes with One Click

Photoshop Elements can help you hide blemishes easily. You can use the Spot Healing Brush to clear blemishes or even smooth out wrinkles and freckles with one click. Adjust the size of the brush for each imperfection and Elements magically makes them vanish with each click.

Remove Blemishes with One Click

① Open a photo in the Standard Edit workspace and duplicate the Background layer as described in the task "Duplicate the Background Layer," earlier in this chapter.

② Click the **Zoom** tool (🔍) and zoom in to the area with blemishes.

③ Click the **Spot Healing Brush** (🖌).

④ Click the **Size** ▸ and move the slider to adjust the size of the brush.

Note: *The brush size should be just slightly larger than the blemish.*

⑤ Click a blemish or small imperfection to make it blend with the rest of the skin.

Note: *You can click and drag on slightly larger imperfections.*

⑥ Repeat Steps **4** and **5** until all the imperfections are removed.

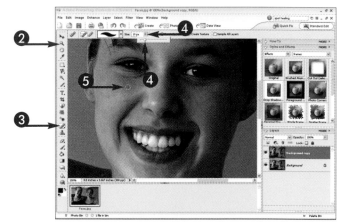

Fix Skin Tone

The new Skin Tone Adjustment in Photoshop Elements brings out more natural skin colors in photos of people. Although the changes are subtle and depend on the individual photo, most images can be quickly improved with enhanced skin tone.

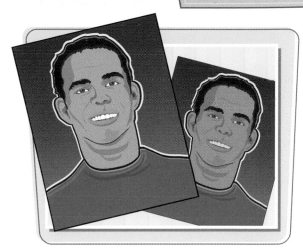

Fix Skin Tone

① Open a photo in the Standard Edit workspace and duplicate the Background layer as described in the task "Duplicate the Background Layer," earlier in this chapter.

② Click **Enhance**.

③ Click **Adjust Color**.

④ Click **Adjust Color for Skin Tone**.

The Adjust Color for Skin Tone dialog box appears.

● Make sure that **Preview** is selected (☑).

⑤ Click an area of skin.

Photoshop Elements makes an automatic correction.

● You can click and drag the **Tan**, **Blush**, or **Temperature** sliders to fine-tune the adjustment.

⑥ Click **OK**.

Getting Creative with Photoshop Elements

After you learn to take great photos and improve them in the digital darkroom with Photoshop Elements, you can use the software to add text to your photos or even turn your photos into text. You can also use the tools and layers in Photoshop Elements to create photo collages or transform your photos into totally new creative images such as paintings or sketches.

Create a Digital Photo Collage

Creating a page filled with different photos is easy using Photoshop Elements. You can determine the size of the finished page depending on the printer you use and the size required for your frame or photo album. Open the photos you want to use. Click and drag the open photos onto the background. The various photos are added as different layers. You can resize them by clicking and dragging their transformation handles and reposition them by dragging them around the page.

Create a Digital Photo Collage

① Launch Photoshop Elements in the Standard Edit workspace.

② Click **File**.

③ Click **New**.

④ Click **Blank File**.

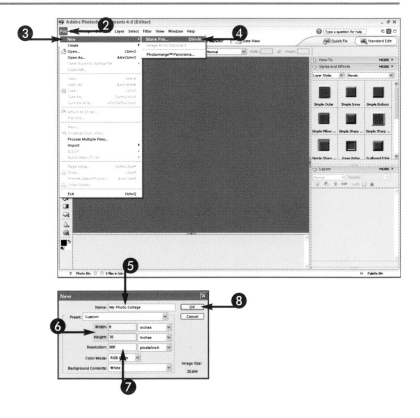

The New dialog box appears.

⑤ Type a name for the collage.

⑥ Type the width and height for the final size of the image.

⑦ Type **300** in the **Resolution** field.

Note: See Chapter 15 for more information on resolution.

⑧ Click **OK**.

A new blank page filled with white appears.

9 Click **Photo Browser** to open the Photo Browser.

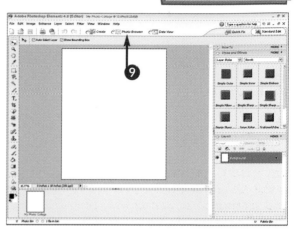

The Photo Browser opens.

10 Press and hold **Ctrl** as you click the photos to include in the collage.

11 Click the **Edit** ▾.

12 Select **Go to Standard Edit**.

TIPS

Can I change the color of the background?

Yes. Scroll to the bottom of the **Layers** palette. Click the **Background** layer to highlight it. Click **Edit** and then **Fill Layer** to open the Fill Layer dialog box. Click the **Use** ▾ and select **Color** to open the Color Picker. Click a color In the Color Picker and click **OK** to close the dialog box. Click **OK** in the Fill Layer dialog box to apply the color to the background.

What else can I use as a background?

You can use any of the patterns included with Photoshop Elements to have a textured background for your photo collage. Click **Edit** and then **Fill Layer** to open the Fill Layer dialog box. Click the **Use** ▾ and select **Pattern**. Click the **Custom Pattern** ▾ and select a pattern from the list. Click **OK** in the Fill Layer dialog box to apply the pattern to the background.

continued

Photo Collages can include the entire photo or a selection from a photo. You can make the selection in the open photo using any selection tools. Click the selection with the Move tool and drag it over the blank page in the Photo Bin. When you release the mouse, only the selection is added as a separate layer.

Create a Digital Photo Collage *(continued)*

The selected photos appear in the Photo Bin.

Note: *If all the photos appear in the main window as individual files, click the **Maximize Mode** icon (⬜) on the menu bar.*

⑬ Click the **Move** tool (▶).

⑭ Click a photo in the Photo Bin to open it in the main window.

⑮ Click the photo in the main window, drag it over the blank page file in the Photo Bin, and release the mouse.

The blank page opens with the photo as a top layer.

⑯ Select **Auto Select Layer** (☐ changes to ☑).

⑰ Press and hold [Shift] as you click and drag a corner handle to shrink the photo to fit on the page.

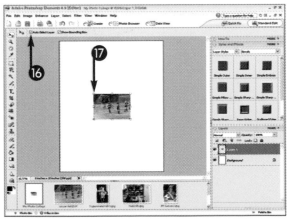

18 Click in the center of the photo to move it into position on the page.

19 Click the **Commit** button (✔) to apply the transformation.

20 Repeat Steps **14** to **19** until all the photos are on the blank background.

21 Click on each photo and then click and drag the handles to make further changes.

Note: See the task "Frame a Photo with a Background Layer" in Chapter 13 to add the bevels and drop shadows shown in the illustration.

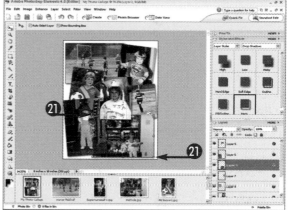

 TIPS

How can I rotate a photo as shown in the illustration?

Using the **Move** tool (⊹), click one of the photos in the collage to bring up the transformation handles. Hover the cursor just outside a corner handle (changes to ↻). The cursor changes to a curved arrow. Click and drag to rotate the photo.

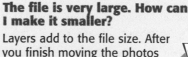

The file is very large. How can I make it smaller?

Layers add to the file size. After you finish moving the photos and adding any styles, you can flatten the image to make one smaller file. Click the **More** ▶ on the **Layers** palette. Select **Flatten Image**. Photoshop Elements combines all the layers into one Background layer. Click **File** and then **Save As** and save the collage with a new name.

What Is the Filter Gallery?

With Photoshop Elements you can apply a variety of filters to improve or change your images. The various filters included with the application can be applied from the Filter menu or the Styles and Effects palette. You can also use the Filter Gallery, which is a more flexible way to visually change your images.

Use the Filter Gallery

Selecting Filter Gallery from the Filter menu opens a new dialog box. The various filters are grouped into folders, and the thumbnails of each filter appear when you open a group folder. Clicking a filter allows you to see a large preview of the effect before you finalize the filter.

Advantages of Using the Filter Gallery

Using the Filter Gallery gives you more control over the effect on the image. Not only can you see a large preview of the effect, you can also apply more than one filter to a photo and see the effect each one has on the overall image. You can add as many filters as your computer's memory allows. You can also use the sliders to change the settings for each filter you apply and click and drag the effects layers within the dialog box to change the order in which they are applied.

Disadvantages of Using the Filter Gallery

Not all the filters included in Photoshop Elements can be applied from the Filter Gallery. When you click **Filter** in the main menu, you see more filters than when you select **Filter** and then **Filter Gallery**. Using the Filter Gallery can also seem slower than just clicking a filter in the **Styles and Effects** palette because opening the Filter Gallery dialog box takes time.

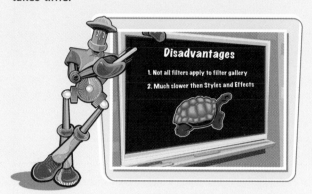

Various Parts of the Filter Gallery

The Filter Gallery dialog box has four separate sections. The preview window on the left opens the photo at 100 percent view. You can zoom in or out using ⊞ and ⊟, click the percentage data field to select a different size, and click directly on the preview image to move it around in the window. The folders containing the thumbnail views of each filter are in the center of the dialog box. The top section on the right includes any adjustment sliders for the currently selected filter. The bottom-right section shows a list of the applied filters as effects layers.

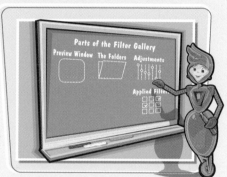

Apply, View, Rearrange, and Delete Applied Filters

Adding multiple filters is one of the major benefits of using the Filter Gallery. Click the **New Effects Layer** icon (▣) at the bottom right of the dialog box to add an additional filter layer. Click a different filter thumbnail to change the type of filter used on that layer. You can alternatively hide and show the effect by clicking the **Visibility** icon (👁) by the layer. Rearrange the effects layers by clicking and dragging them to change the order, and the overall effect also changes. To delete a layer effect, you can click and drag the layer to the trashcan icon (🗑).

Image Size and the Filter Gallery Filters

On the monitor, a very large image file can appear almost unchanged by certain filters. To transform a photo into an artistic image, the filters in Photoshop Elements modify the pixels in the photo. They add texture, displace some pixels, and increase the contrast of others. Because the changes are applied to each pixel, the artistic changes to a large file can sometimes appear minimal on the screen. Always view the final image at 100 percent or full size to judge the effect of the filters on your photo.

Adjust a Photo Before Applying Filters for Artistic Effects

You can increase the artistic look of your image by first cropping it and adjusting the highlights and shadows. You can crop out distracting elements in the original photo using the Crop tool to focus on the area of interest. You can also lighten overly dark areas before transforming a photo into a sketch or painting. The artistic effects of the filters are generally more visible on lighter areas.

Adjust a Photo Before Applying Filters for Artistic Effects

① Open a photo in the Standard Edit workspace.

② Click the **Crop** Tool (◫).

③ Click and drag across the photo to select the area to keep.

④ Click and drag the corner handles to adjust the area.

⑤ Click the **Commit** button (✓).

The photo appears cropped in the window.

⑥ Click **Enhance**.

⑦ Click **Adjust Lighting**.

⑧ Click **Shadows/Highlights**.

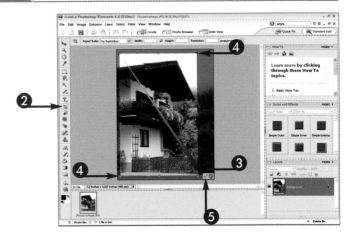

The Shadows/Highlights dialog box appears.

⑨ Click and drag the **Lighten Shadows** slider to the right to see more detail in the shadows.

⑩ Click and drag the **Midtone Contrast** slider slightly to the right to increase the contrasts.

⑪ Click **OK** to apply the changes.

● The dark areas of the photo appear lighter than the original, showing more details.

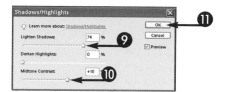

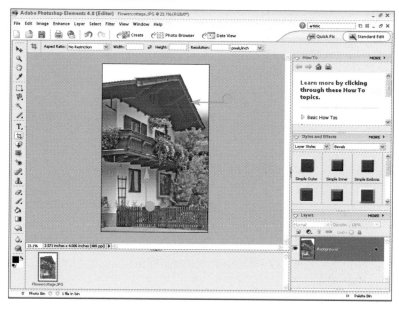

TIPS

When I drag the Lighten Shadows slider, why do my photos look washed out?

Dark shadows may look good on a photograph; however, they become dark, blurred areas when applying an artistic filter. You are changing the image from a photo into a sketch or a painting, so you want the filters to affect all the areas.

Does the file size affect the way the filters work?

Yes. Because the filters modify the individual pixels in the photo, a large file with more pixels has more data to be changed. The filter requires not only more computer memory, RAM, to work on a large file, it also takes more time for the filter effect to appear on-screen and to be applied to the image. When you click a filter in the Filter Gallery, allow the preview screen time to redraw the filtered image. The larger your image size, the slower the filter.

Convert a Photo into a Sketch

You can turn a photograph into a sketch in a variety of ways using Photoshop Elements. The following technique shows one way. You begin by creating multiple effects layers within the Filter Gallery. Each time you change the order in which you apply the filters, reposition the effects layers, or change the slider settings, your sketch has a different style.

Convert a Photo into a Sketch

① Open a photo in the Standard Edit workspace and adjust it as described in the previous task, "Adjust a Photo Before Applying Artistic Filters for Artistic Effects."

② Click **Enhance**.

③ Click **Adjust Color**.

④ Click **Remove Color**.

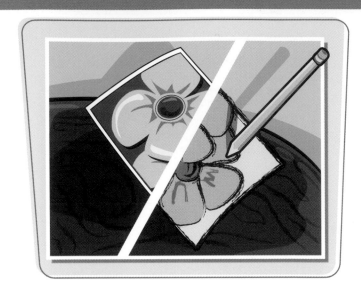

The image changes to a grayscale photo.

⑤ Click **Filter**.

⑥ Click **Filter Gallery**.

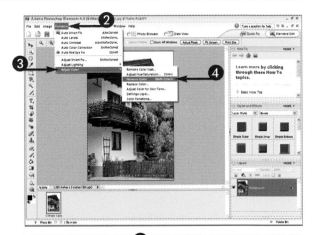

The Filter Gallery dialog box opens.

7 Click the **Brush Strokes** ☑ to view the thumbnails.

8 Click the **Dark Strokes** thumbnail.

9 Click and drag the sliders to make details visible.

10 Click the **New Effects Layer** icon (☐) to add a new effects layer.

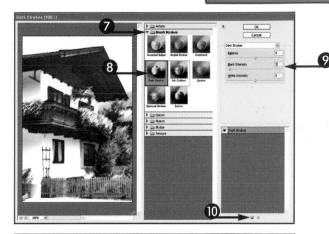

11 Click the **Angled Strokes** thumbnail to change the layer effect.

12 Click and drag the sliders to change the strokes.

13 Repeat Steps **10** to **12**, if necessary, to increase the effect.

14 Click **OK** to apply the filters.

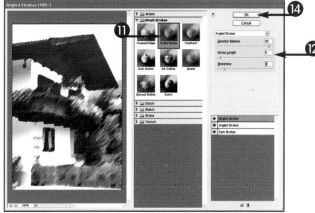

 TIPS

Can I use any of the other Brush Strokes filters?

Yes. Click the **New Effects Layer** icon (☐) and then click any of the other Brush Strokes thumbnails. Each time you add a different brush stroke layer or duplicate an effects layer by highlighting it and clicking the **New Effects Layer** icon, your image has a different look.

What happens if I change the order of the effects layers?

You can click an effects layer in the Filter Gallery dialog box and drag it to a different position in the order of the layers. Because the effects are cumulative, the look changes when you change the order. You can also add as many effects layers as your computer's memory allows.

Convert a Photo into a Painting

Just as with the previous task, "Convert a Photo into a Sketch," there are many ways to change a photo into a painting. You can make your artistic rendering look like a watercolor or an oil painting, and each time you change a particular filter or the order of the layers, the overall painting takes on a new appearance.

Convert a Photo into a Painting

① Open a photo in the Standard Edit workspace and adjust it as described in the task, "Adjust a Photo Before Applying Artistic Filters for Artistic Effects," earlier in this chapter.

② Click **Filter**.

③ Click **Artistic**.

④ Click **Dry Brush**.

The Filter Gallery dialog box appears.

⑤ Click and drag the sliders to adjust the appearance for your photo.

⑥ Click the **New Effects Layer** icon (⬜) to add a new effects layer.

A new effects layer is added with the Dry Brush filter applied.

7 Click the **Texture** 🔽.

8 Click 🔽 and select **Texturizer**.

9 Click 🔽 and select **Canvas**.

10 Click and drag the sliders to adjust the appearance.

11 Click **OK** to apply the filters.

The filters are applied to the photo giving it the appearance of a painted image.

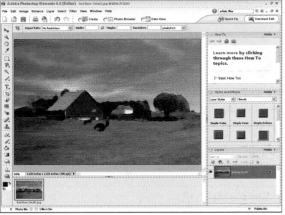

TIPS

Why does my painting lack detail when I use the Dry Brush?

Filters such as the Dry Brush and Palette Knife can change a photo dramatically depending on the size of the brush stroke. If you apply the filters at the default settings, the stroke size can be too high or the stroke detail too low. Click the Effects layer in the Filter Gallery and adjust the sliders.

When I apply the Texturizer, I get a pattern over the image. How can I remove it?

The Texturizer filter applies a texture in the form of a pattern over the image. Click the **Undo** arrow (🔄) and then click **Filter** and **Filter Gallery**. The previous settings should be visible. Try sliding the **Scaling** slider for the Texturizer filter all the way to the right, to 200 percent. Click **OK**. The pattern should not be so obvious.

Finish a Painting with an Artistic Border

Using the Layers palette and the many brushes in Photoshop Elements, you can make a painted photo or any other photograph appear to have been brushed onto a canvas.

Finish a Painting with an Artistic Border

1 Open a painted photo in the Standard Edit workspace.

2 Click the **Create a New Layer** icon (▣) to add a new blank layer above the Background layer in the **Layers** palette.

3 Click **Edit**.

4 Click **Fill Layer**.

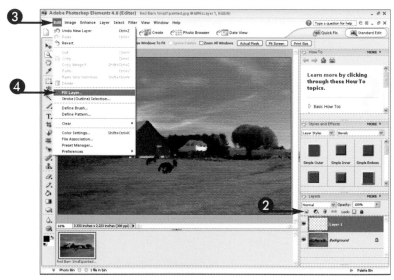

The Fill Layer dialog box appears.

5 Click the **Use** ⊡ and select **White** for the fill contents.

6 Click **OK**.

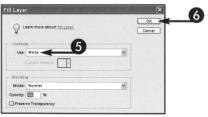

The blank layer fills with white and covers the photo in the main window.

⑦ Click the **Eraser** tool (🗋).

⑧ Click ⏷ to open the Brush Picker.

⑨ Scroll through the Brush Picker and click **Spatter 59 pixels**.

⑩ Click the **Opacity** ▶ and drag the **Opacity** slider to the left until you see the photo underneath.

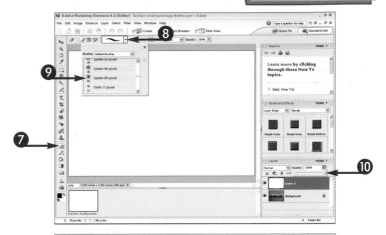

The photo appears beneath a faded white layer.

⑪ Click and drag across the image to erase the central part of the white layer, leaving the edges painted.

⑫ Click the **Opacity** ▶ and drag the **Opacity** slider back to 100%.

TIPS

Where can I find more brushes?

Photoshop Elements includes many other brushes than those in the Default Brushes set. Open the Brush Picker as described in the task. Click the **Brushes** ☑ and select another set of brushes such as **Natural Brushes**. You can also change the size of any brush you pick by clicking the **Size** ▶ in the Options bar and moving the slider.

How can I make the finished image look more like a pencil sketch?

Apply a new blank layer and fill it with white as above. Reduce the opacity of the layer to see the sketch below. Click the **Eraser** tool (🗋) and then click the **Brush** ⏷ and select **Natural Brushes** from the **Brushes** ☑. Select a Stipple brush and erase the white layer using strokes that follow the direction of the sketch lines underneath.

When you add text to a photo or even to a blank new layer, Photoshop Elements adds a special kind of layer called a Type layer. The Type layer contains vector-based text and has a T in the layer thumbnail in the Layers palette.

What Is Vector-based Text?

When you type with a **Type** tool (T), you enter text as vectors rather than pixels. Vectors are graphics composed of lines and curves and are defined mathematically by their geometric characteristics. Unlike pixels that make up a photo layer, the shapes or letters on a vector-based layer can be sized and printed at any resolution and never lose detail or show jagged lines.

Two Ways to Add Text

You can add a single line of text by selecting the **Type** tool, clicking in the image to place an insertion point, and typing the letters. To add a paragraph of text with automatic returns, click and drag a rectangle to create a text box. Then type the letters in the text box and the lines automatically wrap to fit in the box.

Three Ways to Commit the Type Layer

To commit the Type layer, click the **Commit** button (✔) in the Options bar. The Type layer is automatically committed if you select another tool or if you click elsewhere in the image away from the text or text box.

Change the Text on a Type Layer

As long as the text is on a Type layer, and the layer thumbnail in the **Layers** palette has a T on it, you can reselect the text with the **Type** tool and edit the letters or the text color. You can also change the text orientation from horizontal to vertical and even warp the type using the options in the Options bar.

Add Styles to a Type Layer

You can add styles to the text on a Type layer, such as bevels or drop shadows; however, you cannot add filters or effects without converting the vector-based text into pixels. If you change the text on a Type layer, all the styles are applied to the new text. Although you can change the color of the text on a Type layer, you must convert the layer to pixels to color the individual letters differently.

Convert a Type Layer

Converting a Type layer into a pixel-based image layer is called simplifying or rendering the layer. After the layer is simplified, you can no longer edit the letters to change the words because the text is now an image just like another photo layer.

How to Simplify a Type Layer

To simplify a Type layer, click **Simplify Layer** from the **Layer** menu or from the list under the **More** ▶ on the **Layers** palette. You can also simplify a Type layer by highlighting the layer in the **Layers** palette and double-clicking a Filter or an Effect thumbnail from the **Styles and Effects** palette.

Add and Edit Text

When you add type to an image, the Type tool creates a separate Type layer with a T in the layer thumbnail. The individual letters or the complete text on a Type layer can be edited with the Type tool at any time.

Add and Edit Text

1. Open a photo or a new blank document in the Standard Editing workspace.

2. Click the **Horizontal Type** tool (T).

3. Click $\blacktriangledown$ to select a font family.

4. Click $\blacktriangledown$ to select a font style.

5. Click $\blacktriangledown$ to select a font size.

6. Click in the image to set an insertion point.

7. Type the text.

8. Click the **Commit** button ($\checkmark$).

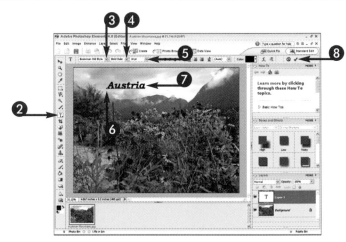

● Elements uses the text you typed as the layer name.

9. Click the type to place the insertion point where you want to add more text.

   You can also click and drag to select the text to change.

Note: If you changed tools after committing the text, click the **Type** tool (T) again.

10. Type the text.

11. Click the **Commit** button ($\checkmark$).

   The layer name changes to the revised text.

You can move the text in the image even after committing it to the layer. You can also resize the text visually without changing the font size in the Type tool Options bar.

Move and Resize Type to Fit

1 Open a photo or a new blank document in the Standard Editing workspace and add text as described in the previous task, "Add and Edit Text."

2 Click the **Move** tool (⊕).

A transformation box appears around the text.

3 Click and drag in the center of the box to move the text.

4 Click and drag on the anchor points of the transformation box to resize or reshape the text.

5 Click the **Commit** button (✔) in the Options bar.

Add Text and Match the Color to the Photo

You can transform any photo into a greeting card by adding text. The resulting image is often more interesting when the text color matches an area in the photo.

Add Text and Match the Color to the Photo

① Open a photo in the Standard Editing workspace and add text as described in the task "Add and Edit Text," earlier in this chapter.

② Click the **Horizontal Type** tool (T).

③ Click the **Type** layer to highlight it.

④ Click ⌄ and select a new font.

● You can also select a new font style or size.

The new font is automatically applied.

⑤ Click here to open the Color Picker for the text.

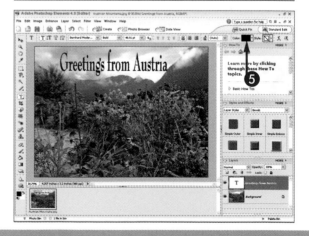

The Color Picker appears.

6 Move the cursor outside the Color Picker
(⟨ changes to ⟩).

7 Click a color in the photo.

8 Click **OK** in the Color Picker.

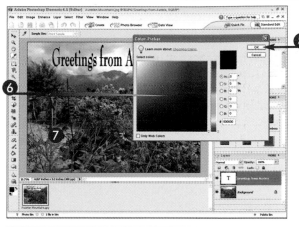

The Color Picker closes, and the new color is
applied to the Type layer.

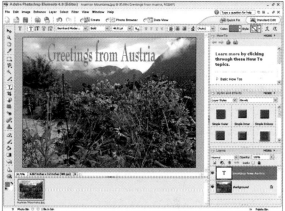

TIPS

**Should I duplicate the Background
layer before adding type?**

Not necessarily. The **Type** tool (T)
automatically adds the type
to a separate Type layer
so your original
Background layer is
not altered until you
flatten all the layers
into one.

**Can I also change the color of the
text with the Foreground color box?**

Yes. As long as the **Type** tool is selected,
and the Type layer is highlighted in
the **Layers** palette, you can
click either the **Foreground**
color box or the **Color**
thumbnail in the **Type** tool
Options bar to open the
Color Picker and change the
color of the text on a Type
layer.

Rotate Text

With your text on a separate Type layer, you can rotate the text to fit your image. You can freely rotate the text or constrain the rotation by specifying the degree amount in the Options bar.

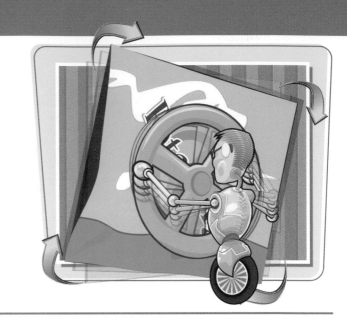

Rotate Text

① Open a photo or a new blank document in the Standard Editing workspace and add text as described in the task "Add and Edit Text," earlier in this chapter.

② Click the **Move** tool (⊕).

A transformation box appears around the text.

③ Position the cursor just outside a corner anchor (↖ changes to ↻).

④ Click once just outside the corner anchor.

The Options bar changes.

⑤ Click here and enter the degree of rotation.

The text rotates.

You can also click and drag to rotate the text freely to suit your photo.

⑥ Click the **Commit** button (✓).

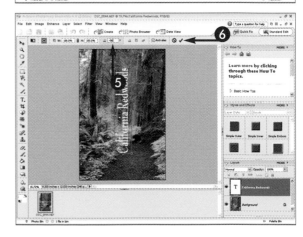

You can warp text to make the letters wrap around a cylindrical form or just to stylize the text. The Warp Text dialog box and the adjustment sliders help you transform the text to any shape you want.

Warp Text

① Open a photo or a new blank document in the Standard Editing workspace and add text as described in the task "Add and Edit Text," earlier in this chapter.

② Click the **Warp** icon (⊥).

The Warp Text dialog box appears.

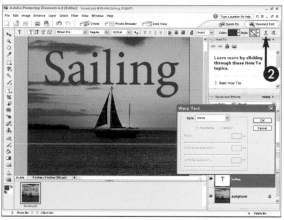

③ Click the **Style** ▾ and select a style.

The default warp values are applied to the text.

④ Click and drag the sliders to adjust the warp.

⑤ Click **OK**.

Add style to any text on a Type layer by clicking one of the Layer Styles in the Styles and Effects palette. You can apply multiple styles as these are cumulative, and you can customize the style by editing the Style Settings.

Stylize Text

① Open a photo or a new blank document in the Standard Editing workspace, add text, and warp as described in the previous task, "Warp Text."

② Click the left ⌄ on the **Styles and Effects** palette and select **Layer Styles**.

③ Click the right ⌄ on the **Styles and Effects** palette and select **Photographic Effects**.

④ Click a photographic effect thumbnail.

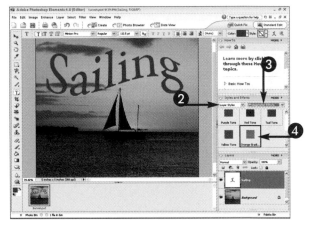

The style is applied to the Type layer.

⑤ Click the right ⌄ on the **Styles and Effects** palette and select **Bevels**.

⑥ Click a Bevels thumbnail.

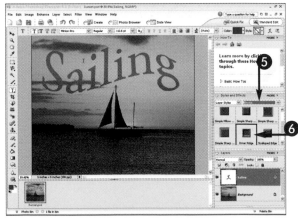

The Bevel style is applied to the Type layer.

⑦ Double-click the *f* icon (◉).

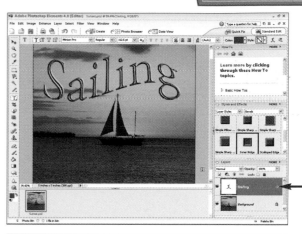

The Style Settings dialog box appears.

⑧ Click and drag the available options and sliders to adjust the style.

Note: *The available sliders depend on which Layer Styles are applied, and not all have editable settings.*

⑨ Click **OK**.

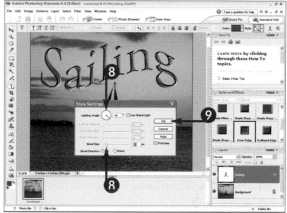

TIPS

How do I remove the Type layer?

You can remove the Type layer by clicking and dragging the layer over the Layers palette trashcan icon (🗑). You can also click the layer to highlight it, click the **Move** tool (▸⊕), and then press `Backspace`. Click **Yes** in the dialog box that appears.

Can I remove the styles but leave the Type layer?

Yes. Click the *f* icon (◉) next to the Type layer and drag it over the **Layers** palette trashcan icon (🗑). All the applied styles are removed, and the Type layer remains as editable type on the layer.

Simplify a Type Layer

A Type layer is not filled with pixels like a photo layer. It is made up of vectors or mathematically defined shapes. Before you can add photo effects and filters to the text, you must convert or simplify the Type layer into a regular image layer.

Simplify a Type Layer

1 Open a photo or a new blank document in the Standard Editing workspace and add text as described in the previous task, "Stylize Text."

2 Click the **More** ▶ on the **Layers** palette.

3 Select **Simplify Layer**.

● You can also click **Layer** and then **Simplify Layer**.

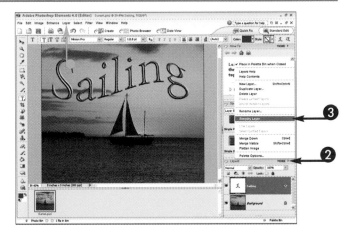

● The text is changed to pixels, and the Type layer thumbnail changes to an image layer thumbnail.

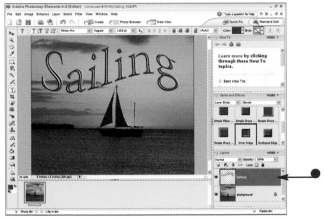

When the Type layer is simplified, you can put the text into perspective. Unlike transformations that are applied to a vector-based Type layer, adding perspective stretches and moves the pixels that make up the text so the edges are fuzzy or pixilated. Make only small changes for the best results.

Put Text into Perspective

① Open a photo or a new blank document in the Standard Editing workspace and add text as described in the previous task, "Simplify a Type Layer."

② Click the layer with text in the **Layers** palette to highlight it.

● You can also click the **Move** tool ( ) and click directly on the text.

③ Click **Image**.

④ Click **Transform**.

⑤ Click **Perspective**.

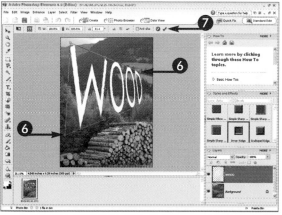

⑥ Click and drag the corner anchor points.

⑦ Click the **Commit** button ( ).

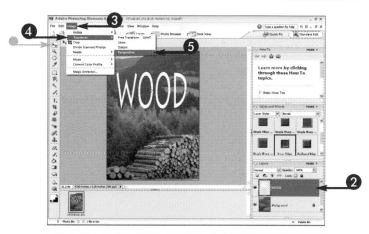

Make a Photo-Filled Text Title

You can fill text with any background or photograph by grouping Type layers and photo layers in Photoshop Elements. Using this grouping technique, the photo shows through only where there are letters on the Type layer below.

① Open a photo in the Standard Editing workspace.

② Click and drag the Background layer over the **Create a New Layer** icon (🖳) to duplicate it.

③ Click the **Type** tool.

④ Click 🔽 and select a font.

⑤ Click in the image and type the text title.

⑥ Double-click the **Move** tool (▶⊕).

⑦ Click and drag the border anchors to stretch the type to fit the photo.

⑧ Click the **Commit** button (✔).

9 Click and drag the Background copy layer and release the mouse above the Type layer in the **Layers** palette.

10 Click the original **Background** layer to highlight it.

11 Click **Edit**.

12 Click **Fill Layer**.

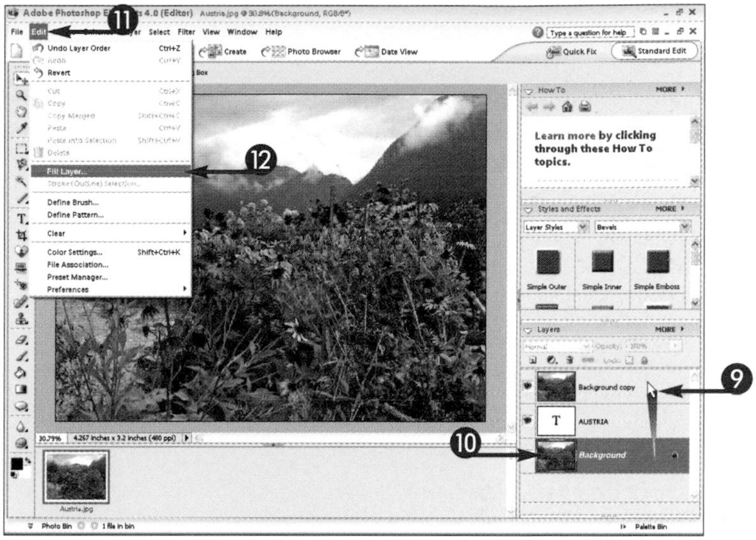

The Fill Layer dialog box appears.

13 Click the **Use** ▼ and select **White**.

14 Click **OK**.

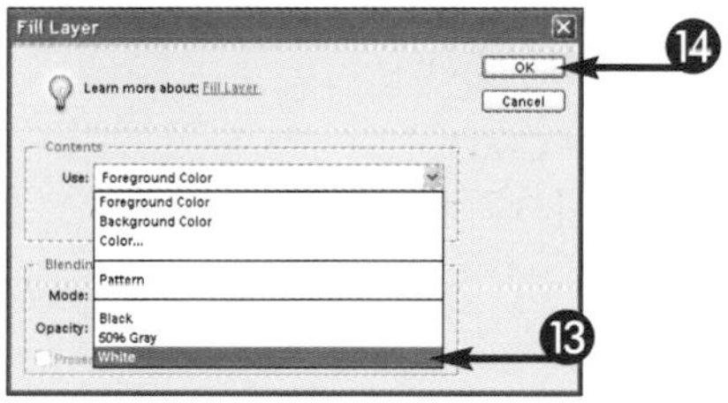

TIPS

What fonts can I use for this effect?

You can use any font; however, a thick font such as Impact or Poplar produces the best results. Also, be sure to stretch the letters with the **Move** tool (▸✥) to fit the photo.

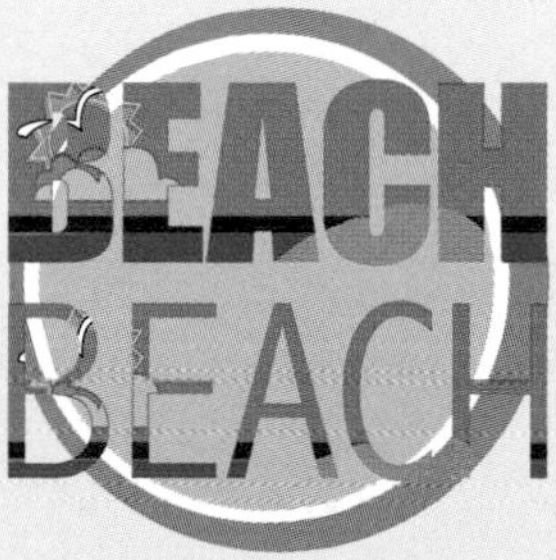

Can I create photo-filled vertical text?

Yes. As long as the text is on a Type layer, you can apply any of the Type tool options including Warp or Vertical type, bold, or italics. You do not need to select a color for the text because it is filled with the photo.

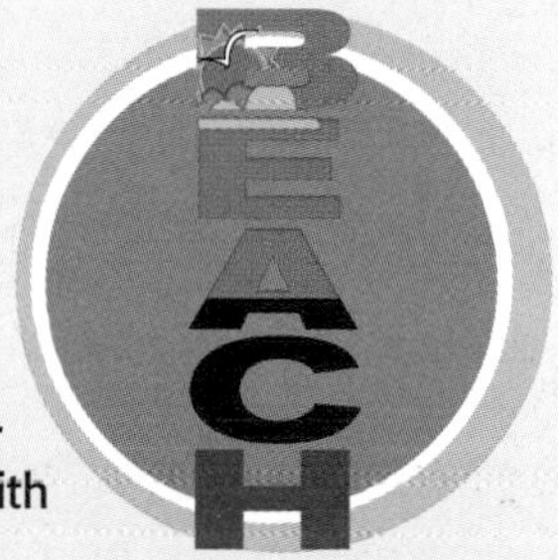

continued

When you group a photo layer with the Type layer below it using Group with Previous, you are creating a Clipping Group. The base layer, in this case the Type layer, defines or clips what is seen from the grouped layer above. The base layer of the Clipping Group appears underlined and the top layer is indented in the Layers palette.

Make a Photo-Filled Text Title *(continued)*

● The original Background layer fills with white.

⓯ Click the **Background copy** (top layer) to highlight it.

⓰ Click **Layer**.

⓱ Click **Group with Previous**.

The photo appears cut out in the shape of the letters.

⓲ Click the **Move** tool (🖰).

⓳ Click and drag in the image to adjust the photo position.

⓴ Click the **Type** layer in the Layers palette to highlight it.

㉑ Click the left ☑ in the **Styles and Effects** palette and select **Layer Styles**.

㉒ Click the right ☑ in the **Styles and Effects** palette and select **Drop Shadows**.

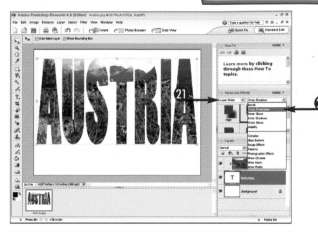

㉓ Click a Drop Shadow thumbnail.

The drop shadow is applied, which makes the photo-filled letters stand out from the background.

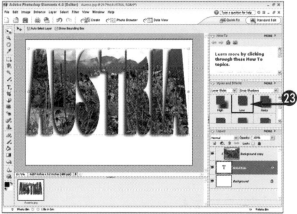

TIPS

Can I readjust the letters?

Yes. You can change the font style, add a warp, or completely retype the text at any time. Click the **Type** layer in the **Layers** palette. Click the **Type** tool (T) and edit the letters as you would with any other Type layer. Click the **Commit** button (✔) to finish editing the text. The photo fills the new text.

Do I have to keep all the layers for a finished file?

No. You can combine all the layers by clicking the **More** ▶ on the **Layers** palette and selecting **Flatten Image**. Be sure to click **File** and then **Save As** to save the photo-filled text with a new filename.

Create a Digital Panorama

Because the human eye can see more than what can be captured in one photo frame, you can let your viewer see a more natural scene by creating a panoramic image from multiple photographs. Photoshop Elements makes combining the photos relatively quick.

Some suggestions for taking the photos: Use a tripod and keep the camera level. Shoot sequentially from left to right or right to left. Keep the same focal length for all the shots. In other words, do not zoom the photos differently. Keep the same exposure for all the shots. Overlap each photo with the previous one by 20 to 30 percent.

Create a Digital Panorama

① Open Photoshop Elements in the Organizer workspace.

② Click to select all the photos to merge.

③ Click **File**.

④ Click **New**.

⑤ Click **Photomerge Panorama**.

*Note: From the Standard Edit workspace, you can choose **File**, **New**, and then **Photomerge Panorama**.*

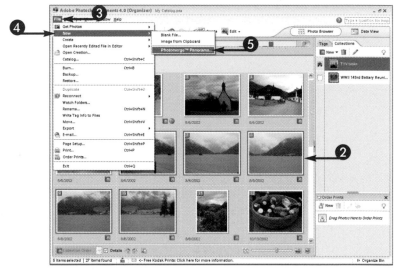

Photoshop Elements opens all the files.

The Photomerge dialog box appears with the open images listed in the data field.

● You can click **Browse** to add other photos.

⑥ Click **OK**.

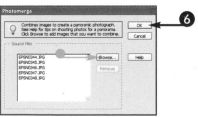

Photoshop Elements attempts to merge all the photos.

● If some or all of the photos cannot be automatically merged, Elements places the thumbnails in the lightbox above the work area.

7 Select **Snap to Image** (☐ changes to ☑).

8 Click and drag to reposition the photos to see if the photomerge improves.

Note: *You can click and drag any thumbnails in the lightbox into the work area to add them to the photomerge.*

9 Click **OK**.

Photoshop Elements merges the photos into a panorama.

10 Click the **Crop** tool (🔲).

11 Click and drag to crop off the uneven edges.

12 Click the **Commit Crop** button (☑) to finish the crop.

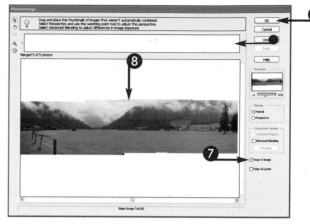

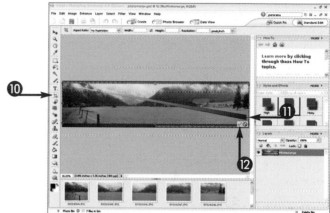

TIPS

What format should I use to shoot a panorama?

If you normally use the Raw format when taking photographs, you can change to the JPEG format when taking photos that are used as panels in a panorama. Each Raw photo must first be converted before it can be used, making the process unnecessarily long. Remember to return your camera to the Raw format after you finish shooting the panorama.

How many photos do I need to make a panorama?

Take as many or as few photos as you need to capture the scene. Just make sure to allow an overlap of about 20 to 30 percent for each shot to give Photoshop Elements areas to line up in the merge process.

Printing Photos and Other Projects

Digital photography is not only a new way to take photos, the way you store and share those photos also differs from traditional film photography. In addition to the benefits of editing and enhancing your photographs, you have more printing options and more ways to share or show off digital images. This chapter covers the basic concepts and introduces you to the many digital archiving and printing possibilities.

Archive Your Photos to CD or DVD Media

With digital photos, your original photo files are your digital negatives. You should always work on a copy of the original file and never alter the original. Photoshop Elements can help you store the original photo files on CD or DVD media to keep them safe. After you edit the copies and make photo creations, you can burn a CD or DVD of those images as well.

Archive Your Photos to CD or DVD Media

① Launch Photoshop Elements in the Organizer workspace and open a catalog.

② Select the individual files to archive.

Note: If you are archiving the entire catalog to CD/DVD, do not select any photos.

③ Click **File**.

④ Click **Burn**.

The Burn/Backup dialog box appears.

⑤ Click **Copy/Move Files** (◯ changes to ◉).

⑥ Click **Next**.

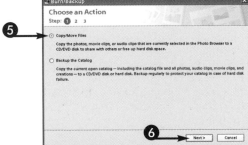

The next screen of the Burn/Backup dialog box appears.

You can leave these options deselected, as in this example.

● Optionally, you can select **Move Files** (☐ changes to ☑) to remove the files from the hard drive for a final backup when your hard drive is full.

7 Click **Next**.

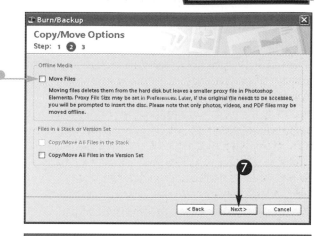

The next screen of the Burn/Backup dialog box appears.

A dialog box appears asking you to insert a blank disc.

8 Insert a blank CD or DVD depending on what type of burner you have.

9 Click **OK**.

10 Type a name for the CD/DVD.

11 Click ☑ and select a write speed for your burner.

12 Click **Done**.

Photoshop Elements calculates the number of discs that are needed and displays a dialog box asking if you are ready to burn the first disc.

13 Click **Burn**.

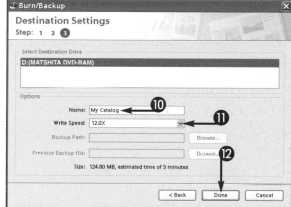

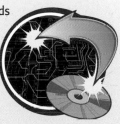

TIPS

How can I label my CD?

You can write directly on the top-side of CD/DVD media with a marking pen. Use only a marker made for writing on CD/DVD media, because the ink from a regular marker can eventually damage the media or the data on the media. Write the name of the disc and the date you burned the disc. You can also print the information directly on special inkjet printable CD/DVD media with some inkjet printers.

A dialog box appears asking if I want to verify the disc. Should I click Yes?

Yes. Verifying a disc adds time to the burn cycle. However, it ensures that the disc is burned correctly. If there is an error, you can burn another copy to be sure all your files are backed up.

Print a Contact Sheet

You can print a traditional contact sheet from Photoshop Element's Organizer workspace. When you print a contact sheet using the photos you select and burn to CD/DVD media, you have a visual record of the images on the media.

Print a Contact Sheet

① Open a catalog in the Organizer workspace and select the photos to print.

② Click **File**.

③ Select **Print**.

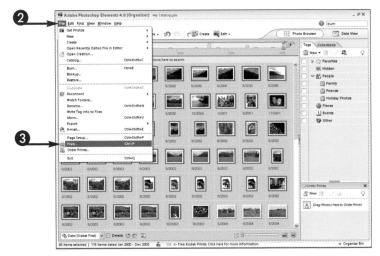

The Print Selected Photos dialog box appears.

④ Click ⬇ and select the printer.

⑤ Click ⬇ and select **Contact Sheet**.

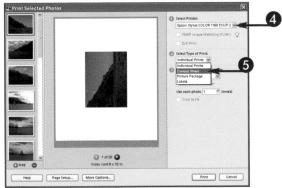

⑥ Click 🔁 and select the number of columns.

⑦ Select these options to add the labels you want to the prints (☐ changes to ☑).

⑧ Click **Page Setup** to set the page size for your printer.

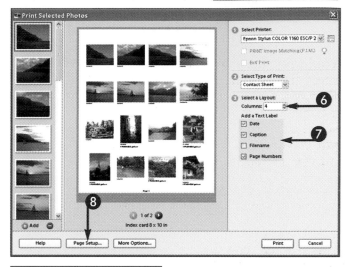

The Page Setup dialog box appears.

⑨ Click 🔽 and select a page size.

⑩ Click **OK** to close the Page Setup dialog box.

⑪ Click **Print** to close the Print Selected Photos dialog box.

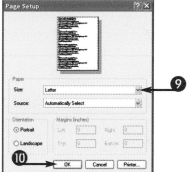

TIP

How do I print a contact sheet that fits in a CD jewel case?
In the Page Setup dialog box, click **Printer**. In the next Page Setup dialog box, click **Properties** and then click **Layout**. If your printer has a CD page size, select it, or click **Custom**. Set the **Width** and **Height** fields to **4.75** inches each. Click **OK** to close each dialog box, and then click **Print** in the Print Selected Photos dialog box. If you cannot set a custom print size, select a small page size from the list. You can print the small page on letter-size paper and trim it to fit a jewel case.

Understanding Resolution

When you take digital photos, view photos on-screen, or print digital photos, the size and quality of the image you view depends on the resolution of the image. The camera, monitor, and printer use different but related types of resolution. Understanding the basic concept is the first step to achieving good quality output from your digital images.

A Basic Definition of Resolution

Resolution refers to the amount of detail you can see in a digital image. Resolution is described as pixels per inch, ppi, on monitors and in images, and as dots per inch, dpi, for inkjet printers.

Monitor Resolution

The monitor's resolution refers to the number of pixels that fit onto the screen. You can set the monitor resolution, such as 1024 by 768 or 800 by 600, in the Display Control Panel. The size of a digital image displayed on-screen depends not only on the pixel dimensions of the image itself and the physical size of the monitor, but also on the monitor resolution settings. An image that is 800 pixels wide by 600 pixels high appears smaller but smoother on-screen when the monitor is set to the higher resolution, because a 1-inch square on the monitor set to 1024 by 768 can contain more image pixels than a 1-inch square on the same monitor set to 800 by 600.

Image Resolution

Unlike film cameras, digital cameras record details as pixels. The larger the resolution capabilities of the camera — as in a 6 megapixel camera versus a 3 megapixel camera — the greater the number of pixels in the resulting image. More pixels in the image means a higher image resolution, and the higher the image resolution, the larger you can print the photo and maintain sharp details.

Printer Resolution

Printer resolution refers to the fineness of details that the printer can reproduce on paper. Printer resolution is measured in dots per inch, or dpi. The greater the number of dots per inch, the finer the detail in the finished print. An inkjet dot can be made up of many droplets, and inkjet printers have different droplet sizes as well as dpi capabilities depending on the model.

PPI Does Not Equal DPI

It is important to understand that the pixels per inch in an image do not numerically equal the printed dots per inch. In other words, the printer does not print a 300-pixels-per-inch image with 300 dots per inch. Inkjet printers may print a 300ppi image at 360 dpi on bond paper, 720 dpi on photo paper, or 1440 or 2880 or higher dpi on the highest grade photo papers.

Best Image Resolution for Inkjet Printing

When preparing an image for inkjet printing, an image resolution of 240 to 300 ppi at the desired width and 240 to 300 ppi at the desired height of the final print is generally considered the standard for the best resulting print.

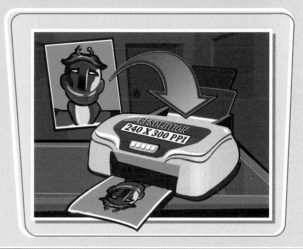

Calculate Desired Print Size by Image Resolution

You can determine the number of megapixels you need to print the best quality photo by multiplying the desired width in inches by the 300-pixel-per-inch resolution, and the desired height in inches by the 300-pixel-per-inch resolution. For a 5-by-7-inch photo, you multiply 5 times 300 to get 1500 pixels per inch, and 7 times 300 to get 2100 pixels per inch. Your camera needs to capture 1500 by 2100 pixels, which is 3,150,000 pixels, or just more than 3 megapixels.

Let Photoshop Elements Figure Out the Size for You

You do not have to break out a calculator. Photoshop Elements can help you determine the largest images you can print without altering the image data. Click **Image**, **Resize**, and then **Image Size**. In the Image Size dialog box, deselect **Resample Image** (☑ changes to ☐). Make sure **Constrain Proportions** is selected (☑). Set the **Resolution** to **300** ppi. The width and height change accordingly, showing the largest print you can make with the best detail from the existing photo.

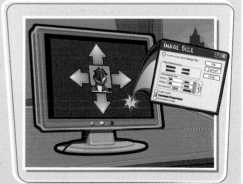

Digital Photo Printing Options

Digital photography offers many different options for getting good prints. You can print photos yourself on a photo printer, take your files to a photo store or kiosk, or use online services. The choice depends on your time and the number of prints you want to make.

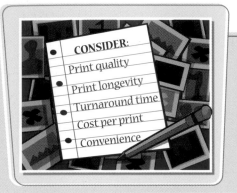

Key Considerations

Whichever option you choose, some of the key factors to consider include print quality, print longevity, turnaround time, cost per print, and convenience.

Print on a Home Photo Printer

If you are printing photographs on your home printer, your printer should be designated as a photo printer. Photo printers generally have more ink colors and can produce prints of various traditional photo sizes. Some use dye-based inks, others specialty dye inks, and others print with pigment-based inks. They can vary in cost from $100 to $600. The cost per print varies from printer to printer and from photo to photo depending on the image itself. In terms of paper and ink, a 4 by 6 photo generally costs approximately 29 cents and an 8 by 10 photo around $3.

Advantages and Disadvantages

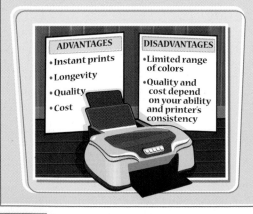

Today's inkjet photo printers offer the instant gratification of seeing your photos printed in front of you and they produce quality prints that can last years depending on the type of ink and paper used, and the way you store or display the photos. Matching the ink and the paper is essential to the longevity and quality of the print. Although inkjet printers that use pigment or UV inks generally make the longest-lasting prints, they may not produce as wide a range of colors as dye-based inkjet printers. Some printers using specialty dye-based inks on the appropriate papers can produce prints rated to last up to 80 or more years. Your average cost per print depends not only on the photo but also on your abilities and the printer's consistency, as mistakes can waste expensive ink and paper.

Print at a Kiosk or a Photo Lab

You can print pictures at photo kiosks, located in photo stores and shopping centers, or at traditional photo labs. Print sizes generally range from 3 by 5 inches to 8 by 10 inches, with varying prices. A 4-by-6-inch photo generally costs around 20 cents with larger print sizes often costing disproportionately more.

Advantages and Disadvantages

You can take your memory card to a kiosk or lab to have prints made. Many kiosks offer basic image editing features such as cropping and red eye removal, giving you the opportunity to enhance your photos before paying for a print. The longevity of the kiosk or photo lab prints vary with the type of equipment the kiosk or photo lab uses to print the photos, although most photo lab prints offer the same print life as traditional photographs.

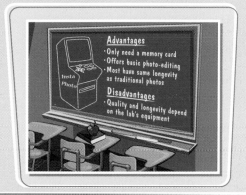

Print at an Online Commercial Photo Lab

You can upload pictures to Web sites, such as Kodakgallery.com and Photoworks.com, which offer commercial photo printing. You simply create an account and upload your digital files. The service stores your photos in online albums. You can select the photos to print and the specific numbers and sizes of each image at any time, and the service mails you your finished prints. Prices can be as low as 12 to 15 cents for 4-by-6-inch prints.

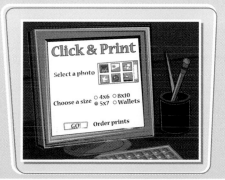

Advantages and Disadvantages

Most online photo labs allow you to share pictures with family and friends for free. Some even send an e-mail to your designated friends when you add photos you would like them to see, offering a new way to share your photos. You or your friends can order prints and even novelty items, such as T-shirts, books, mugs, calendars, and cards with your photos printed on them. Many Web site photo printers use high-quality traditional photo printing techniques so your traditionally sized photo prints last as long as film prints.

Get the Best Prints

Regardless of where or how you print your pictures, you can save yourself time and money by taking certain steps — both in selecting the printing service or printer and in preparing your photos for print.

Evaluate and Test

Print prices and print quality can vary widely with kiosk printers as well as photo labs and online printers. Ask the store or contact the service if they are producing traditional photographic prints or if they are using inkjet or another type of printer. It also pays to obtain sample prints using the same photo from several services and compare the costs and the quality of the prints.

Image Resolution Setting

You get the best results by starting with a high-resolution image file. Set your camera to the highest resolution, which may be called Large, Fine, Superfine, 4 Stars, or something similar. This ensures that the image file size is large enough and has enough resolution to print high-quality photos and enlargements anywhere you decide to print them.

Edit and Enhance Your Photos on a Computer First

Although some kiosks and printing services can crop and make other enhancements to your photos, you can best control the changes and make better decisions yourself using photo-editing software, such as Photoshop Elements. You can be more selective and print only the best photos enhanced the way you want them.

Choose Pictures for Enlargements

Whether you print enlargements on a home printer or use an online or other commercial service, make sure the photos you enlarge have sufficient resolution to be enlarged. Photos with great color, strong composition, and good contrast also make better enlargements. Spend the extra time editing the image carefully and consider making test prints using small areas of the photo to check the results before printing the enlargement.

Crop with Restraint

Because cropping reduces the overall file size, use restraint when cropping photos. The more you crop, the smaller the file becomes, and the smaller the print you can make from the file. Be sure to check the file size in Photoshop Elements before cropping.

Change the File Size

If you leave **Resample Image** selected (☑) in the Image Size dialog box when you change the width and height, you also change the original file size or the original pixel dimensions. When you resample an image, you add or delete image pixels from the image. Changing the pixel dimensions by resampling affects the image quality both on-screen and in print.

When and How to Resample an Image

You may sometimes need to resample images for print, for example to make the photo larger than the original dimensions. For the Web, you almost always need to resample down, or downsample the image to make it smaller so it loads more quickly. Downsampling throws away pixels. When you resample up, Photoshop Elements adds new pixels by interpolation — blending the data from the existing surrounding pixels to create new ones. The final image loses some detail and sharpness.

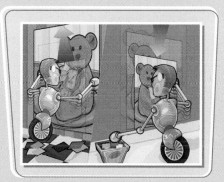

Select Interpolation Methods for Resampling

To maintain the most detail when you need a smaller file size, such as preparing a photo for the Web, leave **Resample Image** selected (☑) in the Image Size dialog box and click ⌄ to select **Bicubic Sharper** for the interpolation method. If you must enlarge the file size, use **Bicubic Smoother**. Remember that Elements is inventing pixels to fill in the added space, so you should avoid overly enlarging the file.

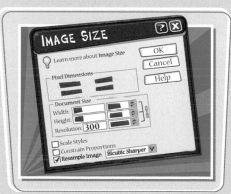

Choose a
Photo Printer

Choosing a photo printer can be educational and fun or downright confusing. Before you begin a search for your personal photo printer, take some time to learn what to look for in a printer so that you can print high-quality photos at home.

Shop for a Photo Printer

Printer manufacturers include so many numbers in the specifications that figuring out what is important or how it compares with another brand of printer can be difficult. First, make sure that you are purchasing a photo printer and not just a color printer. Next, ask yourself what is the largest photo you want to print? The larger the print capabilities, the more expensive the printer. Finally, realize that photo printer technology changes radically every few years. Buy the printer that meets your needs today. You will most likely change printers as the technology improves.

Types of Photo Printers

You can choose from two types of photo printers — inkjet and dye sublimation. Most photo printers today are inkjet printers. Because they are designed to print high-quality photos, they may print more slowly than a printer designed to print text documents. However, inkjet photo printers can be used to print both photos and text. Dye sublimation printers produce very high-quality prints, but the cost per print is much higher than that of inkjet photo printers and they do not print text well.

Inkjet Printers

Inkjet printers spray tiny droplets of ink through a series of nozzles on the print head. The inkjet printers from various manufacturers differ in the technology used to force the ink through the nozzle as well as the type of ink used. Some inkjets use a dye-based ink and others a pigment-based ink. Desktop inkjet printers can print various sizes from 4 by 6 inches all the way up to 13 by 19 inches and longer depending on the brand and the model.

Dye Sublimation Printers

Dye sublimation printers create high-quality, continuous-tone prints that resemble traditional photo prints. They use colored dyes on individual layers of plastic transfer film and use heat to transfer the images to special types of papers. The print sizes are limited with dye sublimation printers and the costs per print are often higher than for inkjet prints.

Printer Resolution

Printer resolution refers to the fineness of details that the printer can reproduce on paper as measured in dots per inch or dpi. Theoretically, the greater the number of dots per inch, the finer the tonal subtleties in the finished print. Select a photo inkjet printer that can print at least 1440 dpi. Higher resolutions are not always better, can consume more ink, and require longer printing times. The human eye often cannot see the difference between a photo printed at 1440 dpi and the same photo printed at 2880 dpi on the same paper. The printer resolution needed to print the best quality photo also depends on the type of paper surface. You might print the same high-quality photo at 1440 dpi on a glossy paper and at 720 dpi on a matte paper.

Printer Speed

Unless you expect to print a large number of photographs, speed is not usually a critical issue. The advertised speeds of the printer often refer to printing one page of text or a low-quality photo multiple times, not several different pages or photos, so the numbers are difficult to interpret and compare.

Print Quality

The most important feature of a photo printer is the quality of the print. Try to collect print samples from the various printer models you are considering and on similar types of paper, such as glossy photo prints from one printer manufacturer and glossy photo prints from another manufacturer, always using the printer manufacturer's own papers. Compare the black areas in the photos. Look at the photos in different lighting conditions to see if the colors change. Pick the printer that produces the print you like best.

Match Prints to Monitor Display

Matching what you see on-screen to what you see in a photo print can be a challenge. Controlling the reproduction of color is called Color Management and is the most difficult part of digital photography.

What to Expect

Prints can never appear exactly the same as what you see on the monitor because the way monitors produce color is different from the way printers produce color.

Monitor Color Versus Printed Color

The screen and printer use different color systems — RGB on-screen and CMYK on the printer. The monitor produces colors by transmitting combined red, green, and blue light sources. We therefore see colors on the monitor as transmissive light. The printer reproduces colors by combining CMYK: cyan, magenta, yellow, and black inks. Many photo printers today print using up to nine colors of ink, with additional variations of CMYK, such as Light Cyan and Light Magenta to increase tonal variations. We see the printed colors as they are reflected off the paper, or as reflected light. When you print the image displayed on-screen, the RGB must be converted to CMYK — or variations of CMYK — and that process is not exact.

Basic Color Management

Professional photographers use a color management system to try to make colors more consistent from camera to monitor to printer. Color Management involves special hardware and software that calculates the color each device produces. The software makes adjustments to match the color space or range of colors a device can produce with an established device-independent standard from the International Color Consortium or ICC.

Set the Monitor Colors

Good color management requires a hardware and software system. You can get close color matches by following certain steps, starting with monitor calibration and profiling as described in Chapter 12. At the very least, use the Adobe Gamma software that comes with Photoshop Elements, or Apple's Display calibration to set your monitor.

Choose the Editing Color Space in Photoshop Elements

Before changing any photos that will be printed, set the working color space. Click **Edit** and then **Color Settings** from either the Quick Fix or Standard Edit workspace. Select **Always Optimize for Printing** (○ changes to ◉) to set the Adobe RGB color space for editing and printing photos.

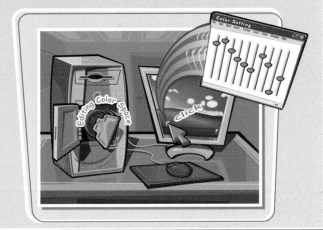

Match the Print Options

Printing on your printer involves two separate print dialog boxes, one for Photoshop Elements and one for your particular printer. When you are ready to print an image, set the print options in Photoshop Element's Print Preview dialog box. When you click **Print** in the Print Preview dialog box, your own printer's dialog box appears. Set the options for your printer and match the paper description to the type of paper you are actually using.

Keep Camera Settings Consistent

You can also get more consistent color by using the techniques provided in this book and by keeping your camera settings consistent. Avoid judging the colors and tones of the photo you just took using the small reviewing screen on the camera. It can only display a very limited number of pixels and colors. Avoid using the camera controls to add saturation or contrast. You can use the more powerful image editing software, such as Photoshop Elements, on your computer.

Optimize Printer Settings and Print a Photo

When you print photos and other images on your personal printer, selecting the appropriate printer settings first can help you get the best results. Although you can print from the Organizer workspace, you have more options for better-quality prints when printing from the Editing workspace in Photoshop Elements.

① Open a photo file.

② Click **File**.

③ Click **Print**.

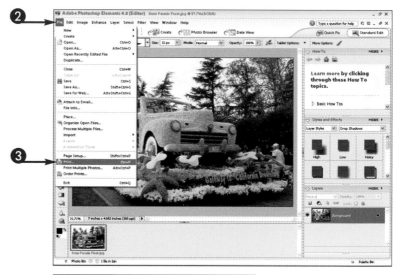

The Print Preview dialog box appears.

④ Click **Page Setup**.

The Page Setup dialog box appears.

5 Click ☑ and select the paper size.

6 Click an orientation (○ changes to ⊙) depending on your photo.

7 Click **OK**.

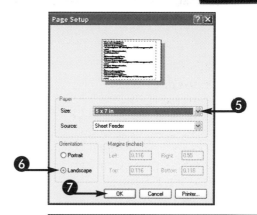

● The settings in the Print Preview dialog box reflect the paper size and orientation you choose.

8 Click **Print**.

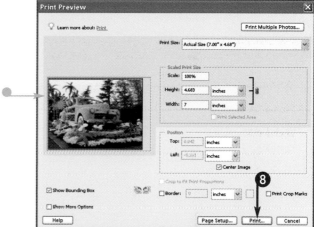

continued

TIPS

Why do I get so many warning dialog boxes when I want to print a borderless photo?

Some photo printers can print so-called borderless photos, images that are printed all the way to the edges of the paper. The warnings indicate that the amount of ink sprayed is reduced as the printer approaches the paper borders. Although this is technically accurate, the changes are generally imperceptible to the viewer. Click **OK** to close these boxes.

Why do I have bands or wide streaks across the print?

Banding lines and streaks on a print can come from using the wrong paper type or thickness, from misaligned printer heads, or from clogged inkjet nozzles. You can use the utility software provided with your printer driver to test and align the inkjet heads and/or clean the inkjet nozzles. You may need to perform a number of cleaning cycles complete with test prints to clear a blocked nozzle.

You should always set the paper type to match the specific paper and print surface you are using. The printer driver can then determine the optimum amount of ink to spray as well as the correct spray patterns to produce the best results on that particular type of paper.

Optimize Printer Settings and Print a Photo (continued)

Note: You may get a Print Clipping Warning dialog box about the paper's printable area. Click **OK** if you are using the borderless feature of your photo printer. Otherwise select **Scale to Fit Media** (☐ changes to ☑) and then click **OK**.

The Print dialog box appears with the name of your printer in the Name data field.

9 Click **Properties**.

Your printer's Properties dialog box appears.

Note: The Properties dialog box and options vary depending on the printer model.

10 Click the **Media Type** ☑ and select the paper type.

11 Select **Print Preview** if the option exists for your printer (☐ changes to ☑).

12 Click the **Paper** tab.

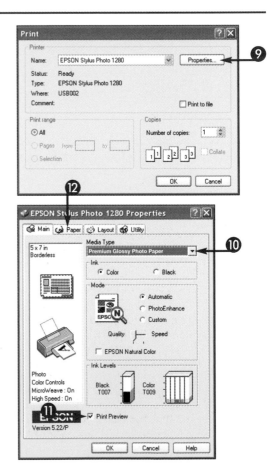

The Printer Properties dialog box displays the Paper options.

⑬ Select **Borderless** (☐ changes to ☑) to make the printer print to the edges of the paper.

Note: If a Borderless warning dialog box appears, click OK.

● You can also select **Maximum** (◌ changes to ◉) to make the printer print as large as possible.

Note: If the Printable Area - Maximum dialog box appears, click OK.

⑭ Click **OK** to close the Properties dialog box.

⑮ Click **OK** to close the Print dialog box and begin printing.

A new Print Preview dialog box appears showing the image as it appears when printed.

⑯ Click **Print**.

TIP

What do I need to know about the Color Management settings in the Print Preview dialog box?

These are advanced settings. If you select **Show More Options** (☐ changes to ☑) in the Print Preview dialog box, the Print Preview dialog box extends. You can select a specific Printer Profile from the drop-down list of the same name. The default is set to **Same as Source**, meaning the printer selects the color space for printing according to the source space of the image, preferably **Adobe RGB 1998**. If you have specific profiles for your printer and paper type, they appear in the drop-down list. By selecting a specific printer profile in the Print Preview dialog box, you instruct Photoshop Elements to control the color through the printing process. You must then adjust the printer's settings so that the printer driver does not add more color adjustments. To do this, click **Print** to open the Print dialog box and click **Properties**. In the Properties dialog box, select **Custom** (◌ changes to ◉) in the Mode (or Color) section. Click **Advanced**. In the Advanced dialog box, select **No Color Adjustment** (◌ changes to ◉), and click **OK** twice to return to the Print dialog box.

Print One Photo as a Traditional Picture Package

You can print various sizes of a photo like traditional portrait studios do, on a single page using your own printer and Photoshop Elements. You can even add frames or borders to customize your photos.

Print One Photo as a Traditional Picture Package

① Open Photoshop Elements in the Organizer workspace.

② Click a photo to select it.

③ Click **File**.

④ Click **Print**.

Click **OK** to close the Printing Warning box, if it appears.

The Print Selected Photos dialog box appears.

⑤ Click ⌄ and select the printer model.

⑥ Click ⌄ and select **Picture Package**.

⑦ Click ⌄ and select a layout.

⑧ Select **Fill Page With First Photo** (☐ changes to ☑).

⑨ Click **Page Setup**.

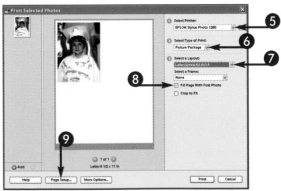

The Page Setup dialog box appears.

⑩ Click 🔽 and select the paper size.

⑪ Click an orientation (◯ changes to ⦿).

● You can click **Printer** to select a different printer and set the Printer Properties.

⑫ Click **OK**.

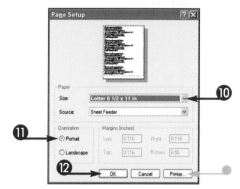

⑬ Click **Print**.

What does the Crop to Fit option do?

When you select **Crop to Fit** (☐ changes to ☑), Photoshop Elements automatically crops each photo so it fits the layout perfectly. A 4-by-6-inch photo used on the layout called **Letter (20) 2x2** is cropped to 2 inches by 2 inches.

What are the Frame options?

You can add a predesigned frame to each photo in the Picture Package by clicking the **Select a Frame** 🔽 and selecting a frame from the list. Only one style of frame can be applied per Picture Package and it is applied to all the photos on the page.

Print a Package with Multiple Photos

You can add multiple photos to one Picture Package to print several different photos at various sizes on the same page. Printing multiple photos on one page and cutting them afterward can save you time and money for paper. You can select all the photos from the Photo Browser at once, or add the photos individually.

Print a Package with Multiple Photos

① Open Photoshop Elements in the Organizer workspace.

② Select multiple photos.

③ Click **File**.

④ Click **Print**.

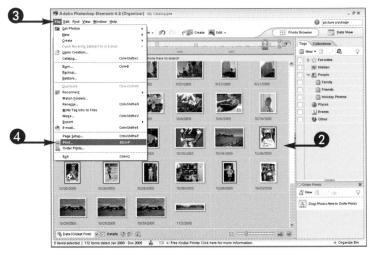

Click **OK** to close the Printing Warning dialog box, if it appears.

The Print Selected Photos dialog box appears with the selected photos on the left.

⑤ Click ▾ and select the printer model.

⑥ Click ▾ and select **Picture Package**.

⑦ Click ▾ and select a layout.

The page fills with the photos in various sizes.

8 Click a photo on the left and drag it onto the page to add it.

9 Click a photo in the layout and drag it over another photo to change the placement and size.

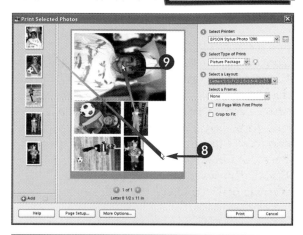

The page layout changes.

10 Click **Page Setup**.

11 Follow Steps **10** to **13** in the previous task, "Print One Photo as a Traditional Picture Package," to print the picture package.

 TIPS

Can I add photos to the layout?
Yes. You can add one or more photos by clicking **Add** ⊕. The Add Photos dialog box appears with the Browser photos. You can click individual photos (☐ changes to ☑) to select them and click **Done** to add them to the layout. Then click and drag them around on the page to place them.

What can I do about the Printing Warning I get when I select certain layouts?
Some of the available layouts are intended for printing on large paper sizes. Click **OK** to close the warning. Then click **Page Setup** and select a larger paper size that is available for your printer. Click **OK** in the Page Setup dialog box. Click and drag the photos from the left side to fill the spaces.

Create a Greeting Card

Using the predesigned templates in Photoshop Elements, you can quickly make photo greeting cards with your photos. You can also add text if you wish to personalize the card. You can create your own thank-you notes, baby announcements, valentines, and more. Then share them easily by printing them, adding them as an attachment to e-mail, or using an online printing service.

Create a Greeting Card

① Open a photo in Photoshop Elements in the Editor workspace.

② Click **File**.

③ Click **Create**.

④ Click **Photo Greeting Card**.

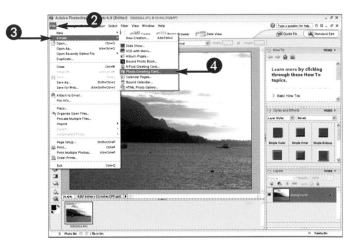

The Photo Greeting Card dialog box appears, showing the Creation Set-up screen.

⑤ Click a card style.

⑥ Click **Next Step**.

⑦ In the Arrange Your Photos screen, click **Next Step** again.

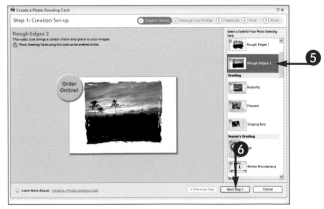

The Customize screen appears.

⑧ Click the corner anchors to adjust the photo.

⑨ Double-click here to open the Title editing box.

⑩ Type the title.

⑪ Click to select a font, style, and size.

⑫ Click **Done** to close the editing box.

⑬ Click **Next Step**.

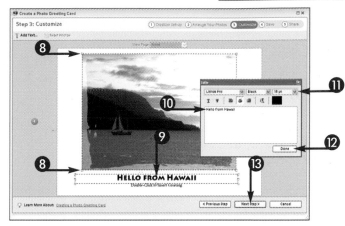

The Save screen with the finished greeting card appears.

⑭ Type a name for the greeting card.

⑮ Click **Save**.

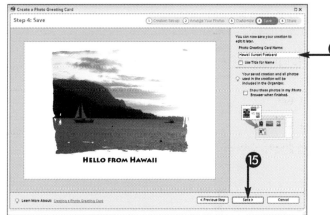

What can I do with a Photo Greeting Card?

When you click **Save**, as in Step **15**, the Share screen of the Photo Greeting Card dialog box appears. You can **Create a PDF** of the card, click **Print** to print the card on your printer, click **E-mail** to send the card directly as an e-mail attachment, or click **Order Online** to print the card using Adobe Photoshop Services through the Kodak Easy Share gallery.

Can I make other Photo Creations the same way?

Yes. You can make slide shows, calendars, album pages, and more using the Create function of Photoshop Elements. From any of the workspaces, click **File**, **Create**, and then select a creation, or just click the **Create** icon ( ) in the shortcuts bar. You can also launch the application directly in the Creation Setup window by clicking **Make Photo Creations** from the Photoshop Elements Welcome screen.

Print to an Online Photo Service

Although printing your digital photos on your own printer is convenient and immediate, it can also be costly and time consuming. Uploading your images to an online service has advantages including being quick and knowing the exact costs upfront.

Fix Your Photos First

Whether you print your own photos or send them out to be printed, you can get the best finished prints by cropping and enhancing the colors and tones of the photos yourself using Photoshop Elements or another photo-editing software.

Use any Online Photo Printing Service

You can save your edited photos in a separate folder to make them easy to find and print. Open your Web browser and log on to any Web-based photo service, such as Photoworks.com, and follow the steps on-screen to upload your photos. Each online service offers a guide and uploading software to help you save and upload your photos to fit their specifications. You can also burn a CD/DVD and mail it to an online service, where they upload all the photos for you. This is very useful if you have a slow Internet connection or numerous photos to upload.

Order Prints from within Photoshop Elements

You can order prints directly from within Photoshop Elements without launching a separate Web browser. Adobe Photoshop Services is linked to Kodakgallery.com.

Adobe Photoshop Services

Click to select the photos you wish to upload from the Organizer workspace. Click **File** and then **Order Prints** or click **Order Prints** in the shortcuts bar. Photoshop Elements prepares the images and opens the Adobe Photoshop Services dialog box. The selected photos are listed along with a number of choices for print sizes, prices, and quantities.

Order Prints and More

Online photo services can print photos at various sizes on different paper surfaces. You can even use the service to help you create and print a variety of photo gifts, such as mugs, puzzles, calendars, cards, books, tote bags, and more. Your items are professionally produced and sent to the addresses you specify.

Set Up an Account

You can open a free account on Photoworks.com, Kodakgallery.com, and many other online photo printing services. You can use your account to upload as many photos as you wish to print or just share online. You can add e-mail addresses for your friends, and the online service can send a personal message to any of them to let them know you have photos ready for viewing and printing. You can create individual online albums for different events and let different friends and family members log on to specific albums.

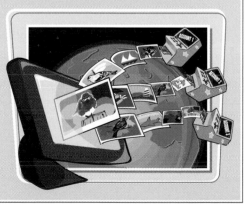

Online Photo Printing Advantages

When you use an online printing service, you know exactly how much each print costs. If you use a high-quality online service, the photographs are printed using equipment similar to silver halide film printing, so you can expect your photos to last as long as traditional film prints. The photo gift items are convenient, and being able to share the photos online and let others purchase their own favorites is an added benefit.

16

Sharing Photos Electronically

Do you want to share your files on the Web or attach them to an e-mail? This chapter shows you how to prepare your photos for online viewing. It also shows you how to safeguard your photos with a personal copyright.

Add a Personal Copyright to Protect a Photo

If you upload your photos to a Web site for viewing but do not want others to use the files without your permission, you can add a personal copyright to the photo. You can make the personal copyright transparent to keep the photo visible but still protected.

Add a Personal Copyright to Protect a Photo

① Open Photoshop Elements in the Quick Fix or Standard Edit workspace.

② Click to select the **Type** tool (T).

③ Select the font family, style, and size you want in the Options bar.

④ Click in the document to set an insertion point.

⑤ Press **Alt** and type **0169** using the number pad on your keyboard.

Note: If you are using a laptop, press **Shift** + **Num lock** to turn on the number locked keys. Then press **Alt** +*mjo9* for 0169.

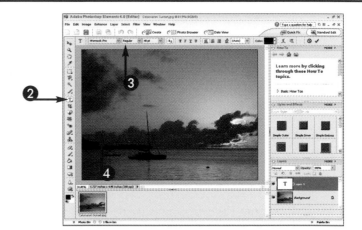

● The copyright symbol appears.

Note: If you are using a laptop, press **Shift** + **Num lock** to turn off the number locked keys.

⑥ Type your name next to the copyright symbol.

⑦ Click ✔ to commit the type.

● The copyright symbol and your name are on a
Type layer above the photo layer.

8 Click the **Styles and Effects** palette ⬇.

9 Click ⬇ and select **Effects**.

10 Click ⬇ and select **text effects**.

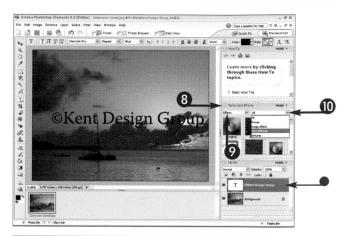

11 Double-click the **Clear Emboss** effect.

● The copyright and your name appear as a
transparent, embossed copyright on the photo.

TIPS

How can I move the copyright to a different location on the photo?

Because your copyright is on a separate layer, you can easily move it to another location on the photo. Click the **Move** tool (⊕) and click and drag in the center of the copyright to move it where you want.

Can I change the size of the copyright?

Yes. Because your copyright is on a separate layer, you can easily change its size. You can cover as much or as little of the photo as you feel appropriate. Click the **Move** tool (⊕) and click and drag a corner of the bounding box around the copyright to stretch the copyright to the size you want.

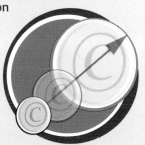

Save a JPEG for the Web

Photo files intended for printing can be large. If you upload this same photo file to the Web, it will appear very slowly on the viewer's screen. Photoshop Elements includes a Save for Web command to automatically save a duplicate of the file in another format that is optimized for Web viewing.

Save a JPEG for the Web

① Open Photoshop Elements in the Quick Fix or Standard Edit workspace.

② Click **File**.

③ Click **Save for Web**.

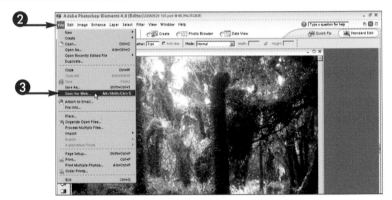

The Save For Web dialog box appears.

④ Click ▾ and select **JPEG**.

⑤ Click ▾ and select a JPEG quality setting.

● Alternatively, you can select a numeric quality setting from 0, low quality, to 100, high quality.

⑥ Check that the file quality and size are acceptable in the preview window.

⑦ Click **OK**.

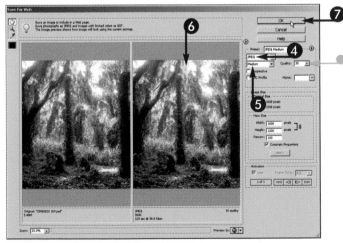

The Save Optimized As dialog box appears.

8 Click the **Save in** ⏷ and select a folder in which to save the file.

9 Type a filename.

10 Click **Save**.

Photoshop Elements saves the JPEG file in the specified folder. You can open the folder to access the file.

● The original image file remains open in Elements.

TIPS

What is image compression?

Image compression applies a mathematical formula to reduce file size. JPEG, the compression method most often used with photos, retains all the color information but deletes some pixels to shrink the file size. You can select the amount of JPEG compression by choosing an image quality setting. Lower quality increases the amount of compression and creates a smaller file. Always edit the photo before you save it as a JPEG. Each time you open a JPEG file, edit it, and save it again as a JPEG, the loss of data compounds, further reducing the image quality.

Why not just use the Image menu to resize the photo file?

The Save For Web dialog box automatically saves the file as a duplicate so you do not risk overwriting your original. It also allows you to preview the different options for optimization specifically intended for Web files in a side-by-side view. The preview image window changes to reflect any changes you make to the settings, such as compression and color options, or the size of the image.

You can use Photoshop Elements for more than just editing and saving digital photographs. You can create illustrations or graphic elements, such as a Web button with text and large areas of solid color, and even design Web animations. For these types of files, select GIF — Graphics Interchange Format — in the Save For Web dialog box.

Save a GIF for the Web

① Open Photoshop Elements in the Quick Fix or Standard Edit workspace.

② Click **File**.

③ Click **Save for Web**.

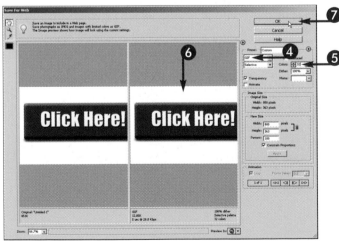

The Save For Web dialog box appears.

④ Click ⏷ and select **GIF**.

⑤ Click ⏷ and select the number of colors to include in the image.

Note: *Selecting fewer colors creates a smaller, faster loading file. Check the preview window to see if fewer colors still shows the image the way you want it.*

⑥ Check that the file quality and size are acceptable in the preview window.

⑦ Click **OK**.

The Save Optimized As dialog box appears.

8 Click ▼ and select a folder in which to save the file.

9 Type a filename.

10 Click **Save**.

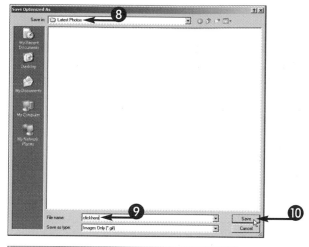

Photoshop Elements saves the GIF file in the specified folder. You can open the folder to access the file.

● The original image file remains open in Elements.

TIPS

If it makes such small files, why not use the GIF format for every image?

The GIF format keeps line art and type sharp but reduces the file size by compressing large areas of color, as in a cartoon, and limits the overall number of colors in the image. JPEG is better for continuous tone photographs because it keeps all the color information even though it somewhat reduces the sharpness of the details in the photo.

Can I create an illustration for the Web and have the Web page background show through?

Yes. When you add type or create a shape in Photoshop Elements, the type or shape is placed on a layer above the Background layer. If you hide the Background layer, you see the type or shape on a gray-and-white checkerboard. The checkerboard indicates transparent areas. To preserve those transparent areas, select **Transparency** (☐ changes to ☑) in the Save For Web dialog box.

Preview an Image in a Browser

Photoshop Elements lets you preview the image in a Web browser so you can see how it will appear to your viewers. You can preview the image in any Web browser you have installed on your computer.

Preview an Image in a Browser

① Open Photoshop Elements in the Quick Fix or Standard Edit workspace.

② Click **File**.

③ Click **Save for Web**.

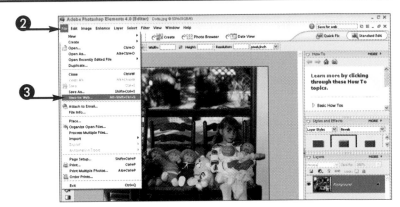

The Save For Web dialog box appears.

④ Click the **Preview In** ▾ and then click **Edit List**.

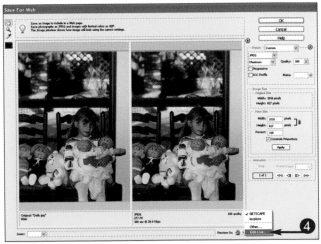

The Browsers dialog box appears.

5 Click **Find All**.

● Photoshop Elements populates the list with the browsers installed on your computer.

6 Click a browser name.

7 Click **Set As Default**.

8 Click **OK** to close the Browsers dialog box.

9 Click the **Preview In** button ().

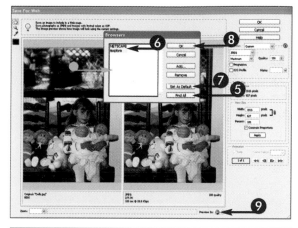

Photoshop Elements opens the default Web browser on your computer and displays the image in the browser window.

● The area below the preview shows general information about the image.

TIPS

Why should I preview the image in various browsers?

Different browsers can make colors appear differently because the various browsers use different color spaces. To make sure your image displays the way you want it to, test it in as many browsers as possible.

What is all the information below the preview image?

Photoshop Elements lists the image file format, the dimensions in pixels, the image size, and compression specifications. It also shows the coded HTML information in the second paragraph, which is the text required to build a Web page with the image.

Create a Web Photo Gallery

You can have Photoshop Elements create a photo gallery Web site that showcases your images. Elements not only sizes and optimizes your image files for the site, but also creates the Web pages that display the images and links those pages together.

Create a Web Photo Gallery

① Open Elements in the Organizer workspace.

Note: For more information about using Organizer, see Chapter 11.

② **Ctrl** +click the images you want to display in your gallery.

If you do not select any photos, Elements displays all the images in your gallery.

③ Click **File**.

④ Click **Create**.

⑤ Click **HTML Photo Gallery**.

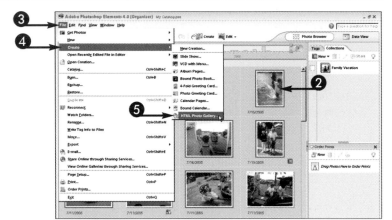

The Adobe HTML Photo Gallery dialog box opens.

⑥ Click the **Gallery Style** ⏷ and select a gallery style.

The style determines the gallery theme as well as how the images are organized.

⑦ Type a title for the gallery banner.

● You can type an optional e-mail address to display in your gallery.

⑧ Click the **Font** ⏷ and the **Size** ⏷ to format the gallery title.

⑨ Type the name of a new folder in which to save your gallery files.

⑩ Click **Browse**.

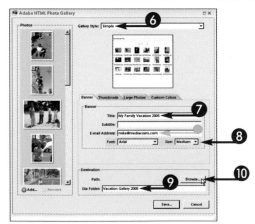

The Browse For Folder dialog box opens.

⑪ Click the destination for your new gallery folder.

⑫ Click **OK**.

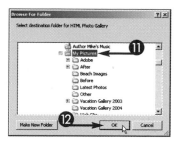

● The folder appears in the **Path** field.

⑬ Click the **Thumbnails** tab.

Thumbnails are the clickable miniature versions of your images in the gallery.

⑭ Click the **Thumbnail Size** ▾ to specify the size of the thumbnails.

⑮ Click these options to select formatting for the thumbnail captions.

⑯ Click these options (☐ changes to ☑) to specify what information will appear in the captions.

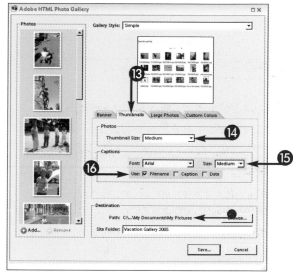

TIPS

How do I determine the number of thumbnails that appear on each photo gallery page?

Photoshop Elements arranges the images on the pages based on the size of the thumbnails. To increase the number of images on each page, select a smaller thumbnail size. To decrease the number of photos on each page, select a larger thumbnail size.

How does the e-mail address appear in my gallery?

The Photo gallery style you choose determines where the e-mail address appears on the page. It may appear below the gallery title, or it may appear below each large image. The e-mail address displayed is clickable; clicking it opens a new e-mail message on the viewer's computer.

continued

When you create a Web photo gallery, you specify the size and quality of the images that display in the gallery. Photoshop Elements creates small versions of your gallery images, which viewers can click to access larger versions.

Create a Web Photo Gallery *(continued)*

⑰ Click the **Large Photos** tab.

⑱ Click the **Resize Photos** ▾ to set the size of the large photos.

● You can drag the ◫ to set the quality of the photos.

Note: Larger and higher-quality images take longer to download over the Web.

You can deselect the **Resize Photos** option (☑ changes to ☐) to keep your images at their current size.

⑲ Click these options to specify the formatting of the larger photo captions.

⑳ Click these options (☐ changes to ☑) to specify what information is used for the captions.

㉑ Click the **Custom Colors** tab.

㉒ Click a color box.

The Color Picker appears.

㉓ Click a color.

㉔ Click **OK**.

㉕ Repeat Steps **22** to **24** for each color in the gallery.

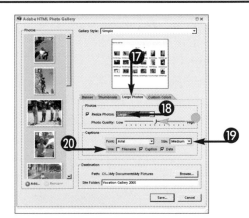

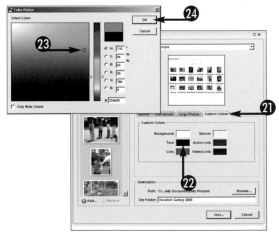

26 Click **Save**.

● Photoshop Elements closes the Adobe HTML Photo Gallery window and builds the image and HTML files for the gallery.

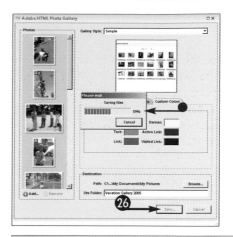

Photoshop Elements opens the completed gallery in the HTML Photo Gallery Browser window.

The window displays how the gallery looks in a regular Web browser, such as Microsoft Internet Explorer or Netscape Navigator.

You can click a thumbnail to view a large photo.

TIPS

How can I view my Web photo gallery as it will appear in a regular Web browser?
You can launch your Web browser and then open the index.html file located in the folder you specified in Step **9**. You can typically click **File** and then **Open** to open a file on your computer using your browser. The index.html file represents the home page of your Web photo gallery.

How do I get my gallery on the Web?
Photoshop Elements creates a folder with all the parts required for a Web gallery page and includes the HTML code. You can upload this folder to your Internet service provider using a Web publishing application such as Adobe GoLive or Dreamweaver, or you can use another file transfer protocol (FTP) software from your Internet service provider.

Sharing your photos with your friends and family is easy. You can use Photoshop Elements to automatically attach an image to an outgoing message in your computer's e-mail program.

This feature requires that you already have an e-mail program, such as Microsoft Outlook or Eudora, set up on your computer. Photoshop Elements does not come with e-mail capability.

Send an Image with E-mail

1 Open Photoshop Elements in the Organizer workspace.

Note: For more information about using Organizer, see Chapter 11.

2 `Ctrl` +click to select the images you want to send.

3 Click **File**.

4 Click **E-mail**.

*Note: Photoshop Elements may display a window asking you to choose your e-mail client. If so, choose the software with which you prefer to send e-mail and click **Continue**.*

The Attach Selected Items to E-mail dialog box appears.

5 Click **Edit Contacts**.

The Contact Book dialog box appears.

6 Click **New Contact**.

The New Contact dialog box appears.

7 Type your recipient details.

8 Click **OK**.

● The recipient appears in the Contact Book.

9 Click **OK** to close the Contact Book.

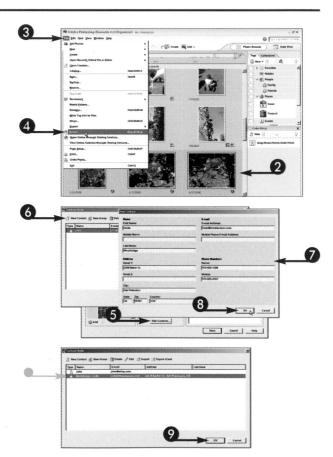

- In the Attach Selected Items to E-mail dialog box, click to select one or more e-mail recipients (□ changes to ☑).

10 Click the **Format** ▾ to select a format for your e-mail.

You can send your images as attachments, embedded in your message (Photo Mail), or as a slide show.

11 Select the size and quality settings.

Note: These settings may differ depending on the chosen format.

12 Type a message.

13 Click **Next**.

*Note: If you selected **Photo Mail (HTML)** in Step 10, the Stationery & Layouts Wizard appears. See the tip below for details.*

Photoshop Elements opens a new message in your e-mail client software.

- The recipient is added to the **To** field, and your message text is included in the message field.

Note: For more information about sending your message, see the documentation for your e-mail application.

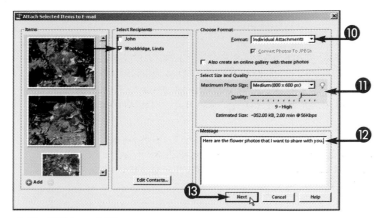

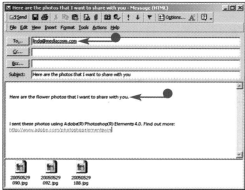

TIP

Can I customize my e-mail with themes?

You can access various templates that add graphical themes to your messages with the Photo Mail (HTML) style.

1 Click the **Format** ▾ and select **Photo Mail (HTML)**.

2 Click **Next**.

3 In the Stationery & Layouts Wizard that appears, click a stationery style; you can view the stationery in the main window.

4 Click **Next Step**.

When you click **Next** in the window that follows, Elements adds the layout to your e-mail message.

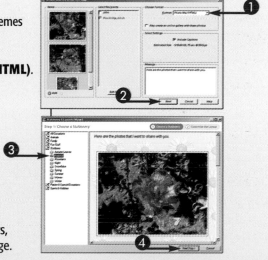

You can export the images in Organizer to a folder in a different location on your hard drive or on a separate hard drive for backup purposes. The original file remains in the catalog and you can export the photos at various sizes and in different file formats.

Export Images

① Open Photoshop Elements in the Organizer workspace.

② Click **File**.

③ Click **Export**.

④ Click **To Computer**.

● If you have a mobile phone connected to the computer, you can click **To Mobile Phone** to move a copy of the selected photos directly to the phone. Photoshop Elements resizes the files appropriately.

The Export Items dialog box appears.

⑤ Select a **File Type** option (○ changes to ◉).

● Some file types allow you to specify a size or quality.

⑥ Click **Browse**.

The Browse For Folder dialog box appears.

7 Select an export folder.

8 Click **OK**.

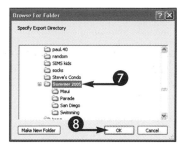

9 Click **Export**.

Elements exports your images.

The Exporting Files Complete dialog box appears telling you how many files were exported.

10 Click **OK**.

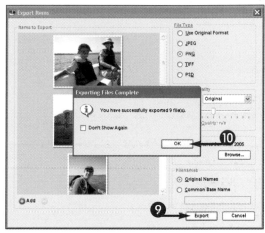

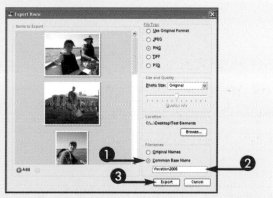

TIP

How do I customize the names of my exported images?

You can customize the filenames of your exported images in the Export Items dialog box:

1 Select the **Common Base Name** option (○ changes to ●).

2 Type a base name for your photo filenames.

3 Click **Export**.

Elements exports your images.

It appends a hyphen and number to your base name to create each filename.

Index

Index

Index

Index

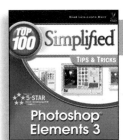

...all designed for visual learners—just like you!

Master VISUALLY®

**Step up to intermediate-to-advanced technical knowledge.
Two-color interior.**

- 3ds max
- Creating Web Pages
- Dreamweaver and Flash
- Excel VBA Programming
- iPod and iTunes
- Mac OS
- Optimizing PC Performance
- Photoshop Elements
- QuickBooks
- Quicken
- Windows Server
- Windows

Visual Blueprint™

**Where to go for professional-level programming instruction.
Two-color interior.**

- Excel Data Analysis
- Excel Programming
- HTML
- JavaScript
- PHP

Visual Encyclopedia™

Your A to Z reference of tools and techniques. Full color.

- Dreamweaver
- Photoshop
- Windows

For a complete listing of Visual books,
go to wiley.com/go/visualtech

Visual
An Imprint of ⓦ**WILEY**
Now you know.

Want instruction in other topics?

Check out these

All designed for visual learners—just like you!

Read Less–Learn More®

Visual®

Teach Yourself VISUALLY™
Adobe® Photoshop® CS2
0-7645-8840-0

Teach Yourself VISUALLY™
The Fast and Easy Way to Learn
Windows® XP
2nd Edition
* Covers Windows XP Service Pack 2!
0-7645-7927-4

Teach Yourself VISUALLY™
Knitting
Sharon Turner
0-7645-9640-3

For a complete listing of *Teach Yourself VISUALLY*™ titles and other Visual books, go to wiley.com/go/visualtech

Visual®
An Imprint of WILEY
Now you know.